GLOBALISATION FRACTURES

HOW MAJOR NATIONS' INTERESTS
ARE NOW IN CONFLICT

Charles Dumas

PROFILE BOOKS

First published in Great Britain in 2010 by
Profile Books Ltd
3A Exmouth House
Pine Street
London EC1R 0JH
www.profilebooks.com

Typeset in Times by MacGuru Ltd
info@macguru.org.uk
Printed and bound in Britain by
Bell & Bain Ltd

A CIP catalogue record for this book is available from the British Library.

ISBN 978 1 84668 424 1

Mixed Sources
Product group from well-managed
forests and other controlled sources
www.fsc.org   Cert no. TT-COC-002769
© 1996 Forest Stewardship Council

Contents

Figures and tables

Acknowledgements

Most of the ideas in this book came out of work on the global economy for Lombard Street Research. I owe my colleagues a huge debt for the constant discussion and analysis of ideas, scenarios and forecasts – particularly Brian Reading, whose original work on the flows of funds is a primary tool employed in this book. He also has helped keep the emphasis on the damaging role of fixed or managed exchange rates – between China and the United States, and within the euro zone – as a vital mechanism by which China and Germany have pursued beggar-thy-neighbour policies for the past decade. Our Lombard Street associate, Leigh Skene, also contributed vital analysis of mortgage and other derivatives. I have gained much from discussions with Martin Wolf of the *Financial Times* and specific important points about Japan from Andrew Smithers. The long-run information and analytical style of Bob Shiller of Yale University have also been helpful. When it comes to economic theory, I have adopted a pick-and-choose approach to the ideas of John Maynard Keynes, Joseph Schumpeter and Milton Friedman, each of whose approaches has great value in thinking about our new crisis.

The managing director at Lombard Street Research, Peter Allen, aside from his pithy summaries of key issues, has shown his usual insight in helping in the choice of title for this book: 'globalisation fractures' is a phrase that not only summarises the hard-to-mend but not completely broken state of the world economy, but was a useful reminder that globalisation itself is broader and more important than the crisis, making it that much more crucial that the world economy is rebalanced. The staff at Profile Books have been monuments of good humour and patience, putting up with sometimes dilatory deliveries from this author, and I am grateful for that. Lastly, I would like to thank my partner, Pauline Asquith, for reading the text with close attention, leading to significant improvements.

Introduction

Who was to blame? That's what we all want to know.

'Nobody and yet everybody' is not too far from the truth, though it will not do. But the range of factors contributing to the crisis was large enough to make a politician's rant worse than useless. Consider a few candidates:

1 The Lehman bankruptcy. This was certainly a precipitating event, and arguably a tactical policy mistake. But the Lehman bankruptcy alone could never have caused the worst stockmarket sell-off in history. The world financial system was a fragile house of cards for deeper reasons, virtually certain to collapse at some point. Without Lehman having been put into bankruptcy, some other event would have triggered a crash.

2 The 'banksters'. The bankers did many things they should not have, and some committed crimes. But most were pursuing their interests in good faith and as approved by the ruling ethos of society, including the constraint of competitive pressures. Bankers will be bankers – and if money is easy they will make money lending it, borrowing it and quite a lot else besides.

3 Hank Paulson and Ben Bernanke. Certainly, the conduct of US monetary and financial policy from mid-2007, when the subprime crisis became evident, contributed to the extreme fragility of the system a year later – and to the disgraceful lack of preparation by these two chief policymakers for full-blown crisis. But the fundamental global imbalances were in place by mid-2007 – the author had been forecasting a US household debt crisis since 2004. Most of the pain that has been gone through – and has yet to come – was unavoidable by mid-2007.

4 Alan Greenspan. By his mental acrobatics he managed to perfect a mental phenomenon: asymmetric ignorance. He always knew when falls in asset prices might be about to cause trouble – and responded with easy policy. But he proclaimed the impossibility of knowing when the 'irrational exuberance' of asset prices might cause trouble! Yet in the context of 2002–03, with the stockmarket down nearly one half after the tech-bubble burst, easy policy was right. And throughout the run-up to the 2007 crisis, the US enjoyed reasonable growth and low inflation – the precise mandate of the Federal Reserve Board (Fed). So who can blame him? Or at least him alone?

5 US government incentives to owner-occupation. To ascribe financial crises this far back up the chain of cause and effect verges on the ridiculous, but some of the more zealous US libertarian economists, as well as political camp followers, have tried it. ('The Bush administration was powerless for seven years, you see, and the whole thing goes back to Clinton-era housing policies.')

6 US, British, Spanish, etc, household borrowers. These are also sometimes called voters, so politicians do not blame them, and sometimes media customers, so neither do journalists and other commentators, for the most part. But a large swathe of people borrowed money they knew they would be unlikely ever to be able to repay. So even on the borrowing side, the blame is beginning to be spread quite thinly.

7 Rating agencies. Which group of alchemists was it that turned lead into gold? The investment bankers with their opaque, indecipherable alphabet soup of innovations get fingered much of the time, but it was rating agency sign-offs that gave AAA ratings to securities that subsequently sold at 25 cents in the dollar; and BBB (investment-grade) securities that became virtually worthless. And who hired them? Investment bankers, of course.

8 China. A nice big target, this one – and the largest on the lender side. It takes a stupid lender to make a bad loan. The problem with the Chinese was that they had other things in mind. They had a view – open to dispute, but hard to argue with considering how rapidly China has developed – about export-led growth being the best way forward, especially after watching South Korea and others being spanked in 1998 for getting into deficit.

9 Japan. Surely, after 20 years of letting the export cycle dominate their virtually growth-free economy, the Japanese authorities should have realised that stimulating the six-sevenths or so of their economy that is domestic demand might be an option. But no: the original savings-glut country and world's second largest economy just carried on being a dead weight on the world.

10 Germany. What can you say about a country that pursues budget-balancing virtue at the expense of killing off its growth, and tries to force the rest of Europe to follow suit, spreading blight across much of a continent?

11 China, Japan and Germany together. The rest of the world could have handled any one of these countries with structural surpluses, but when world economies 2–4 all want large surpluses, it hardly comes as a surprise that spending their money caused some people to overstep the mark. It was more the combination of all these countries wanting surplus than their individual policies that caused problems. But could we really expect them to co-ordinate and limit their aggregate surplus, sharing it out equitably?

It took misconceptions and mistakes by borrowers, intermediaries, lenders and policymakers to create this crisis – spiced up with a sprinkling of criminality and drizzled with the confusion of global interaction. This book will examine:

- the background 'shock' of globalisation;
- the roots of the crisis one by one and in relation to one another;
- the development of the crisis from mid-2007, interactively in the economies and the financial markets;
- the prospects for economies and markets;
- what needs to be done – and probably will not be.

*

Debtors have had a bad rap historically. It is not so long since the penalty was prison. And there are sound reasons why people should be penalised for using someone else's money and then failing to repay. Hence the reductive approach: debt is bad.

Savers, by contrast are good. Some German commentators on the crisis have explicitly referred to themselves as 'saints' and the Anglo-Saxons as 'sinners'. The Book of Genesis (in the Bible) gave us the seven fat years and seven lean years, with the virtuous course being to save up in the fat years to survive the lean ones. Jesus also praises provision for future emergencies in his parable of the wise and foolish virgins. And the wise virgins do not bail out the foolish ones, who have insufficient oil to keep their lamps going when the bridegroom is late: going off to replenish, they get shut out. No moral hazard there. But his tone becomes more mixed when the father's mercy towards his prodigal son arises, and in the parables of the lost coin and lost sheep. The message shifts from the need to save to the need to be prudent, which can have very different implications. And the correct response may not only temper justice with mercy, but also take account of the empirical, utilitarian goal of making things better rather than worse. This point comes across most clearly in the parable of the talents, in which the servants who take the money entrusted to them and double it are praised, and the one who buries it in the ground to conserve it is chastised. How, one might conjecture, does a servant double the money within the span of his master's travels? With a little debt leverage, perhaps – or at least a strong appetite for risk.

*

The crisis was a debt crisis. Nobody doubts that. The initial force destabilising world financial markets was the mid-2007 US sub-prime mortgage slide. The immediate consequence for money markets was the interbank market seize-up. In the year-later crash after the Lehman bankruptcy, no bank was trusted to be able to meet its obligations. Throughout, the issue was potential bad debts – default. Most people were surprised by what happened, including many who should have seen it coming. The search has been on ever since for an explanation of this surprise – someone to blame. The desire for simplicity – more pejoratively, the obsession with sound bites – makes that a search for the cause, in the singular. Preference for a person over an abstraction led on to a search for the person, or group of people, to blame.

This book, following on from earlier papers and books from 2004 to 2008 forecasting such a debt crisis (see Bibliography) will not find any single cause, or group of people, country, or group of countries, to blame. The interesting and insidious thing about this crisis is that most of the relevant groups, countries and groups of countries were behaving reasonably in relation to legitimate and genuine goals and priorities. The multiple causes of the crisis reflected the interaction of groups and countries behaving in ways that, considered in isolation, were reasonable in and of themselves. Crucially, most proposals to modify behaviour patterns or policies that were causing the debt bubble to inflate involved weakening or abandoning these legitimate goals and priorities – and were thus inherently unlikely to be adopted before the emergence of visible ill effects.

This book will therefore direct its focus away from trying to decide who was to blame and towards understanding the multiple causes of the crisis. This involves examining the multiple strands of economic development, policy and behaviour over the past 25 years at least, to trace how the globalised debt bubble became inflated, and the complex consequences of its bursting. In a capital transaction, we expect to have a borrower, a lender and an intermediary. When a deal goes wrong, all have usually made a mistake – excluding cases of fraud (and sometimes not even them, as we shall see). And in cases of major collective errors involving a whole nation, or group of nations, government policy often has biased private behaviour towards what turn out to be mistakes.

Future histories of the years from the early 1980s to 2007 (and, it is hoped, the future) will probably treat them as dominated not simply by the run-up to the recent crisis, but as the second great era of globalisation (the first being about a century earlier). The lifting of an estimated 1 billion people above the poverty line and the associated shift of power to emerging economies have been the most important developments. But this globalisation has introduced instability to relationships within economies that were previously stable; it has permitted fluctuations away from the (sometimes wrongly presumed) equilibrium or mean to be far more extreme than would be feasible in a national-economy context. The very flexibility granted by globalisation takes away or weakens traditional constraints. And in the continuing global crisis, resolving our difficulties must involve a degree of co-operation, or at least mutual forbearance, that may prove difficult.

In the debt crisis of 2007–09, several long-standing developments came together to turn what had been compatibility of divergent behaviour and policy into conflict:

1 **The leveraging of America.** Domestic debt grew at about the same pace as nominal GDP in the 25 years from the end of the Korean war until 1980. But after that it rose rapidly relative to GDP, with a break in the early 1990s, until the crisis – which essentially arose because private-sector debt had seriously exceeded affordable limits. Britain, Australia, Spain and other peripheral European countries saw similar trends.

2 **The primacy of Wall Street.** The faster growth of debt than GDP both caused the financial sector to boom and was itself hastened by financial innovations and soaring financial sector intra-leverage (partly debt, partly derivatives).

3 **Japanese/north-central European demographics and restructuring.** Weak demographics led to high savings and lesser investment needs. Restructuring of businesses to pay down debt

generated yet more surplus cash flow. These countries increasingly depended for their income and asset build-up on ever-mounting deficits and debt in other countries.

4 China and Asian Tigers' mercantilism and backward banking systems. After the shock of the 1997–98 Asian crisis, the already strong conviction that export-led growth was the way to develop a modern economy was reinforced by fear of deficits. Meanwhile, inadequate financial systems and weak social security induced high household savings as well.

For as long as the US private sector was happy to run up its debt load, these four developments were complementary – or appeared so. Wall Street could run riot, and in the general buoyancy of markets, few minded their excessive gains. The excess savers – groups 3 and 4 above, generators of the Eurasian savings glut – required counterpart spender–borrowers to prevent their deficient demand leading to deflation; they were provided with net exports to sustain income growth in the absence of adequate domestic demand, and with assets arising from the debt run-up in the deficit countries. The domestic debts of the US and other deficit nations mounted, in parallel with the inflow of surpluses from the savings gluttons, and therefore so did the unstable financial imbalances of the globalised world economy.

The technical economic and financial turning point was in late 2005 and early 2006, when US house prices, having moved from boom to bubble, peaked. As they started down, the growth of the key deficit-country asset values ceased. This had been the essential underpinning for the previous unbalanced, unstable equilibrium. Yet US policy and Wall Street conduct remained blithely unchanged. The debt bubble continued for another year and a half, creating a huge extra load of poor-quality, overpriced paper to ensure that the crisis, once it came, was considerably worse than it need have been.

At a deeper level, the run-up to 2006 both created the momentum for these end-of-era excesses and had already taken asset values and debts well beyond sustainable levels. And that crucial, 2004–06 period was dominated by the supply-push of excess savings in the savings-glut countries – accounting for ever-shrinking credit spreads and Greenspan's famous 'conundrum' of falling US Treasury yields in the middle of a financial boom and against a Fed that was tightening monetary policy. So while the 2006–07 finale can largely be attributed to US policies and behaviour, the earlier phase was, in true cause-and-effect terms, dominated by the excess supply of savings arising from points 3 and 4 above.

So everybody had an alibi. US policymakers can be blamed for inadequate regulation of banks and excessive encouragement of mortgage loans to borrowers with doubtful credit ratings, but the basic condition of the economy appeared fine, even in mid-2007. The Keynesian/monetarist consensus in favour of on-trend growth with modest inflation was adhered to. In just the good period of the last cycle, after the 2001 recession and before the recent recession, the US economy grew at only 2¾% annually, less than its long-run average. The inflation rate was about the same: 2.9% a year for the total, and 2.1% for the core rate that excludes food and energy prices. The US enjoyed reasonable growth and moderate inflation, the chief goals of demand management. The output gap never exceeded 1%, so the economy was not overheated, and inflation never became a significant problem.

Yet the achievement of such results required a run-up of

debt that made the recent crisis, or something like it, inevitable. For every extra dollar of nominal GDP in the ten years to 2007, private-sector non-financial debt rose by $2.50, or $3.30 when government deficits are added in. Continuation of this form of development ensured that private non-financial debt headed upward towards 250% of GDP, or 330% with government included. So the crisis came, and it blew the whistle on this approach to growth when the private ratio reached 180% in 2007, triggering the subprime crisis and the credit crunch.

Until then capital markets gave no serious alarm signals, as the downward pressure on yields and spreads from the savings glut seeking an investment home meant that debt and debt securities that should never have been created were gobbled up willingly. Action to check the growth of debt would have appeared to be a gratuitous generation of unemployment in a stable and benign economic and financial situation.

Many would argue that the bankers have no alibi, and certainly there was plenty of fraud, and there will be plenty of expensive lawsuits to settle. But a banker's job, as bankers perceived it and as society perceived it, was to maximise income. Savings gluttons were pouring cheap money into the financial markets, so bankers devised ever more elaborate ways of diverting it into their own pockets. The excesses of bankers – pursuing the creation of mortgages and the alphabet soup of associated derivatives to the bitter end in 2007 – probably contributed to the severity of the crisis, but for the most part their behaviour reflected the human norm in the face of large rewards and no constraints. Distasteful, yes, especially with hindsight, but neither illegal nor outside the realm of what was regarded as acceptable at the time.

As for the savings-glut countries, whereas their behaviour

collectively was probably the chief driving force behind the debt bubble over its last five years (2003–07), each of them had good reasons for the policies adopted that promoted the glut – with the arguable exception of Japan – and each of them would be entirely without responsibility for what happened, were it not for all the others attempting the same thing: to grow by generating a large net export surplus. What mattered chiefly was not that Japan, Germany or even China ran increasing surpluses, but that the collective current-account surplus of the savings-glut countries, $1¼ trillion in 2007, was more than three times that of even the largest individual country surplus (by then, China's). With China, Japan and Germany as numbers two, three and four in the world economic pecking order, the collective impact of their aligned policy was huge.

*

Adam Smith may have modified Christian morality by making a qualified case for the value of selfishness, but he did so subject to the requirement of a specific framework: 'peace, easy taxes and the rule of law'. His broadening of the Christian analysis to include these societal conditions – tough ones, in fact, that have been far from fully realised in practice – also modifies the concept of prudence in an economic context, and with it the 'good versus bad' opposition of saving and borrowing.

In the Keynesian scheme of things, what appears to suit a firm, for example cutting wages, may be damaging for all (including that firm) if applied generally throughout the economy, if aggregate income falls and with it demand and profits. Similarly, what seems prudent for an individual – or even an individual country – may not prove prudent if too widely practised. In the modern world economy, an apparently prudent saver may ultimately prove to be imprudent, even assessed from the most narrow, selfish standpoint. And in the process of saving too much, the globalised economy and system have been strained, with reduced willingness to sustain globalised markets, especially free trade, on which savers, especially saving countries, depend.

In the debacle of 2007–09 starting with the credit crunch, the initial problem was with borrowers. As many borrowers had gone ahead with strong encouragement from bankers – the intermediaries – the latter were also held to blame for the breakdown of their ability to repay. The lenders lost a lot of money and were indignant about these losses. Lending countries suddenly found themselves unable to generate their accustomed surpluses, as the former borrowers were immobilised by the credit crunch. They ended up suffering worse recessions than the deficit countries, ratcheting up their indignation further. But not only were they foolish in their individual lending decisions that led to losses; as countries they were also foolish to rely for income and capital accumulation on countries borrowing well in excess of a reasonable credit limit. Since folly is self-evidently not prudent, such saving cannot be regarded as prudent either, and certainly not as an unqualified 'good thing'. It must be for a useful purpose to be prudent, or good, and which purposes are useful are sometimes not known until after the event.

The reasoning above should be largely uncontroversial to economists. Yet the economic establishments of most countries, and certainly those of the savings-glut countries, have concurred with popular and political opinion in focusing almost entirely on the follies of the debtors, and the venality or outright corruption of the intermediaries. This may be helpful in creating rules that make a recurrence of private-sector debt excesses less likely in future. But the argument of this book will be that a healthy recovery of the world economy from the crisis will chiefly depend on two things:

- measures to ensure rapid growth of consumption in savings-glut (surplus) countries, and hence a lesser savings glut;
- measures to improve the flow of such savings glut as remains to optimal investments in the rest of the world.

Both these conditions are about behavioural and/or policy change in the savings-glut countries, not in the debtor countries. The fact that it is chiefly savings-glut countries that need to change their habits suggests that their actions were the cause of the crisis. Yet so far the saver countries have largely failed to acknowledge the contribution to the crisis of their national policies and attitudes. The conclusion will be that such measures are likely to be at best inadequate. In this case a modest and relatively short world economic recovery will be followed by a relapse into renewed crisis or crises, with an eventual satisfactory outcome far from certain.

I

The fundamental 'shock': globalisation

If the roots of the crisis were various behaviour patterns and national policies, as described below, the soil in which those roots were planted was an earth rotovated by globalisation. A relatively balanced OECD economy in the late 1980s had capital and labour reasonably in proportion to one another other, and the inflationary excesses of the 1970s had been driven into retreat by the tight money of 1979–82. Onto this was grafted first the former Soviet bloc and, more importantly, entry into the global free market of some 1¼ billion Chinese and over 1 billion Indians, with the parallel emergence of the Pacific Asian Tigers among others. The bargaining power of western labour was reduced, as were the world's capital assets per potential worker. This has been tough on low-income labour in rich countries. It also under-pinned huge gains in value of existing capital assets (stocks and real estate). High-income labour as well as wealth-holders in rich countries benefited from these gains.

Globalisation was a triumph of the idea of free markets – that is, of capitalism versus various versions of state-directed economic development, some communist or socialist, some merely *dirigiste*. To define the point by its opposite, Japan has been the most conspicuous economic failure of the past 20 years, with its top-down, elitist system. Within Europe, more than vestigial *dirigisme* has hindered core continental economies that have fallen back relative to the US, whereas the readier acceptance of free markets in Britain has caused its relative income to increase – even after taking account of the recent crisis.

The free market principle, however, is a stern master – a jealous god that requires complete obedience. This has not been forthcoming, even in the US. A completely free-market world economy would entail full mobility of:

- goods trade;
- services trade;
- capital;
- labour.

On the whole, countries have sincerely accepted free trade in goods and services and made great progress in its implementation, with clear exclusions, notably agriculture. But countries with cheap labour, such as China, or the prospect of cheapening their labour by tough domestic action, such as Germany, have managed to make the playing field far from level by means of partially fixed exchange rates. They liked free access to other countries' markets, but not the free movement of exchange rates that is needed for it to be sustained, that is, consistent with continued global equilibrium. The cleanest acceptance of global free markets has been in the flow of capital, dominated as it is by American financial principles – and principals – as well as the desire for it in such bastions of saving as Japan, where freedom to invest its huge financial wealth anywhere offers some compensation for the failures of the home economy. But even American acceptance of full capital mobility is far from total, and the newly emerging developing economies seldom fully open up their economies, or even capital markets, to foreign capital.

Where mobility has remained particularly heavily qualified is of course in human beings. This is not the place for analysis of this issue, but it is useful to see how it relates to other aspects of globalisation. Consider some of the elements, circa 1990:

- huge inequalities of income and wages;
- tremendous productive capital assets in advanced countries with their total population of 800–900 million, versus very little in over-a-billion-strong India, or China – a quarter as large again as India – and even in the smaller and less effective emerging countries like Russia, Indonesia, and so on;
- relatively free trade outside agriculture;
- largely immobile populations with ultra-mobile financial capital capable of creating liquidity in any asset under the sun (not to mention some that turned out not to exist).

Meanwhile, Americans indulged their exaggerated sense of invulnerability after the success of the cold war, which encouraged the belief that anything they really want they can have, whatever the apparent constraints of historic reality; and that risk has no downside, and is in effect an opportunity without cost.

Most results of this globalisation 'shock' were highly positive, one being a massive investment boom in response to such high returns on assets – a boom that would provide China, India and eastern European countries with capital assets, transferring technology and raising their average incomes. But major blockages slowed development, which is tragic because but for these block-ages there would be plenty of highly profitable usages for all the savings the world could muster, and no Eurasian savings glut. Western countries and governments would not have needed to induce deficits to dissipate these savings in borrow-and-spend – and would not have been able to without inflation.

The obstructions to adequate growth in the former Soviet bloc are too complex to detail here. In China, the government's control of the energy sector (with price controls as well), the financial sector and fundamental conditions in the housing sector, together with general problems of corruption and the rule of law, severely hobble growth outside the privileged export sector. Impressive though real GDP growth has been, with an annual trend of 10%, it should have been higher – or, more importantly, better balanced towards the consumption needs of ordinary Chinese people. India, as well as being restricted by poor infrastructure, has restrictive labour and agriculture laws that hold back the man-ufacturing sector and many services. These have ensured that the country with the poorest labour on earth has had, in manufactur-ing, capital-intensive rather than labour-intensive growth. Ten-year average GDP growth has accelerated to 7%, but it should (given other factors) be close to 10%.

For a variety of reasons outlined in Chapter 2 and Appendix 2, mature, slow-growth economies with little inward migration in Europe and Japan have savings to spare after meeting their investment needs. In an ideal world – or even a modestly rational one – such savings would capitalise the emerging economies, to their benefit and that of the advanced-country investors. But in the world of the past decade, the savings rate of the most dynamic portion of the emerging world, Pacific Asia, has far exceeded its (or any possible) investment rate; and that of India has only been used up by spectacularly wasteful government deficits, with little resultant overseas deficit. Restating this high saving less euphemistically: very poor people have had the improvement of their standard of living seriously held back.

With all these disparate and mismatched elements, it is small wonder that the world economy has lurched from boom to bubble to bust. And the creative energy of the globalised financial system has increasingly been diverted from benefiting the economy towards papering over the cracks. In particular, as the excess of savings confronted a dearth of profitable permissible uses, it flowed uphill by crowding out savings in the country with the greatest faith that the future would take care of it – the United States. Why save when all is possible to those who dare? The crisis has defined the limits of something-for-nothing in America, and the limits of saving without well identified purpose elsewhere.

Perhaps the most peculiar negative feedback in globalisation arises precisely from its greatest merit: global, rather than national or regional, flexibility in the use of resources. This flexibility has enabled errant behaviour to persist much longer than would have been possible in a more local context. It has nurtured denial. Excessive household debt and a housing bubble were identified early in the 2003–04 US recovery by numerous sceptics. Yet the availability of capital from all over the world proved their warnings wrong for years, so that the go-for-broke rash crowd gained confidence that the good times could go on for ever – that there were no limits. The manufacture of artificial investments by investment banking snake-oil salesmen for the foolish oversavers of Germany and north-central Europe, Japan and developing Asia enabled them to pursue the delusion of never-ending export-led growth with virtuous accumulation of assets.

How many times have we heard analysts say that some statistical variable was 'five standard deviations' from the mean (or some such number)? Yet no ill consequences appeared. Globalisation's first flush appeared to make the unsustainable sustainable. Except that it turned out it was not, and the grey-beards were (at least partly) right all along. In analysing the US debt bubble (see Chapter 2), the excesses will be seen to have served constructive purposes, even though they went too far. But it was globalisation that enabled them to go so much too far.

Globalisation was and is like a form of freedom – freedom at least of trade and capital movement, and to a greater extent than before of people. But it is well known that freedom can only survive with responsibility – if people understand the rules, often unwritten rules. But the initial burst of globalisation encouraged the idea that there are no rules, no limits. We stretched the system until it snapped.

Globalisation has fractured itself. Can it be mended? This book analyses the intense difficulty of a way out of the mess. The situation is not beyond remedy. But it is hard to be optimistic about the outcome.

2

The roots of the crisis

The leveraging of America, 1982–2007

I have previously identified the Eurasian savings glut (as dubbed by Ben Bernanke in March 2005) as the driver of global imbalances in my book *The Bill from the China Shop* (spring 2006). My earlier Lombard Street Research *Monthly International Review* (No. 243, September 2004), *US balance sheets serially trashed by Eurasian surplus* was the original statement of the idea. Coming six months before Bernanke's paper, which introduced the phrase 'savings glut', my review article, as may be seen by its title, forecast the trashing of US household balance sheets by the savings glut (following on the damage to business balance sheets in 1998–2001) and foresaw the future fallback on government borrowing after a household debt crisis. The largely reactive role of (chiefly) American borrowers was proven by the persistence of low real interest rates throughout the 2004–07 debt bubble, and low margins for the extra risk of non-government borrowers. It followed, under that analysis, that persistence (and increase) of the savings glut would require ever more debt to be taken on by Americans that would eventually break them – not as a nation unable to finance its imports, but as an aggregate of overleveraged individual borrowers.

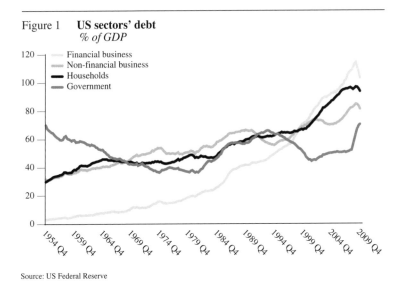

Figure 1 **US sectors' debt**
% of GDP

Source: US Federal Reserve

However, although economic cause-and-effect suggests supply of capital – that is, savers – as the driving force behind the debt crisis, the reality is more complex. As US house prices stopped rising at the end of 2005 and then declined continuously, the capacity of US households for extra debt was non-existent to negative in the last year or two of the bubble. So the take-up of mortgages that depended for future repayment on continued house price increases (Ponzi-style) was clearly delinquent behaviour. Much the same was true of the 2006–07 surge in private-equity transactions taking firms private at low equity cost by loading them up with debt. And the avoidance of traps by investors' due diligence was hampered by opaque securities bearing good ratings from apparently reputable rating agencies, as well as by structural opacity in hedge funds. This opacity may have been a by-product of the banking intermediaries' ever more elaborate search for hidden value, or it may have been at least partly deliberate on their part. Either way, it is their responsibility.

But sceptics had been bewailing the leveraging of America since early in the 25-year debt cycle that started after the 1982 recession, and in some respects earlier. While the forward lurches of the borrowers and their banker handmaidens were certainly enough to arouse alarm – and caused a genuine, recessionary crisis by 1990 – the prophets of doom were both hopelessly premature and arguably seriously mistaken. The recent crisis was indeed caused by US private-sector debt growing too large relative to incomes. But when the current, probably five-year or more, phase of deleverage is over, debt ratios to income are unlikely to have fallen back more than a third of the way from 2007–08 peaks to their 1980 starting points.

Prematurely crying wolf lost the debt sceptics their credibility. As importantly, it ignored major benefits that the increased debt ratios entailed. First, the scope of owner-occupation in the housing market was significantly extended. Second, the rebalancing of business balance sheets away from equity towards debt arguably put pressure on businesses to cut costs, and thus helped cause the substantial upswing of productivity growth between the 1970s and 1980s and the most recent decade.

In analysing the roots of the crisis, it is necessary to examine the whole US debt cycle that started after the twin recessions of 1980 and 1982 had stamped out inflation. This will show how the initially healthy pursuit of risk reduction through diversification led to an increase in domestic debt capacity that genuinely improved welfare, especially as the ebbing of inflation was reflected in lower nominal interest rates, boosting housing affordability. While it was clear to many of us at the time – and everybody now, in retrospect – that the escalation of debt from 2005 onwards was an unsustainable excess, it was also a natural extension of what had previously been a profitable trend. Such is the way with supply-side cycles: first fresh growth, then ripe maturity, followed by morbid excess.

The financial innovations that gathered pace in the 1980s and 1990s tended to spread risk, improve hedging potential and arbitrage away market discrepancies. The result was both a more efficient use of capital by its users and, given easier diversification of risk, greater debt capacity for any given perception of acceptable risk (on the part of either borrower or lender). This was true of foreign-exchange hedging that took away some of the uncertainties from foreign trade, given floating exchange rates, and swaps that enabled a flow of payments on one basis, such as fixed rates over ten years, to be transformed into a different flow, such as a floating rate linked to six-month interbank rates.

At the same time, households for sure, and firms in many cases, are constrained in their borrowing by the simple burden of current debt interest (and, especially with households, repayment). As inflation peaked in 1980, interest rates went far up into the teens. Even real interest rates, that is, nominal rates less inflation, were quite high, once Paul Volcker, as the new Federal Reserve Board (Fed) chairman, moved to stamp out inflation from 1980 onwards. The 1980s and 1990s saw a dramatic reversion of nominal (and even real) rates, falling back to levels not seen since the early 1960s after the stockmarket bubble burst in 2001–02. As a result, the annual financial burden of any given level of debt fell sharply. As this reduced some of the foremost risks associated with debt, an assumption of unchanged appetite for risk implies an increase in debt. But when that increase then did not prove damaging, the appetite for risk itself increased, redoubling the upward surge of debt/income ratios.

The ultimate point is that debt ratios got somewhat out of hand in the late 1980s, owing to the still quite high interest rates then, but only spun seriously out of control in the 2004–07 period. To see how excessive they have become – and assess the need for deleverage – the household and business sectors must be examined separately.

US household debt build-up and impending cut

The ratio of household debt to GDP rose somewhat in the post-second world war recovery until the early 1960s, and then levelled off until 1983. Its rise in the 1980s and (more modestly) the 1990s was during a period of rapidly falling nominal interest rates, as inflation subsided. As well as benefiting from the boost to housing affordability arising from the fall in nominal interest rates (on mortgages), the rise in debt and house prices reflected an important prior asymmetry between incomes and house prices. Real household incomes in the US have risen over time. (Some argue that this is not true of wages, but it is definitely true once account is taken of the increased ratio of two-earner households.) However, real house prices fluctuated around a constant trend level from the end of the Korean war in 1953 until the late 1990s – a level that had been reached at the turn of the 19th century, before the two world wars with the intervening Depression took their toll. These numbers are based on the Case-Shiller index of US house prices, using deep research by Bob Shiller, a professor at Yale University.

Rising real incomes and constant real house prices made a steady contribution to increased affordability. This led home

Figure 2   **US household debt and interest payments**
% of personal disposable income

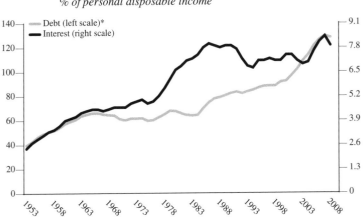

*Differs from Figure 1, as the denominator here is disposable income, not GDP.
Source: US Bureau of Economic Analysis

ownership in the US to rise from around 43–46% in 1900–40
to 55% in 1950 and 62% in 1960. But inflation and therefore
nominal interest rates started their long increase in the 1960s, and
the ratio reached only 64% in 1970, there to stagnate until 1990.
Affordability is driven by three factors: income, house prices and
interest rates. The last of these has the largest effect over anything
but the long term. High nominal interest rates offset the rising real
income ratio to house prices until 1990. But from 1990 onwards,
rising real incomes were reinforced by falling nominal interest
rates. House prices rose as a result, as gains in affordability fed
through. Also rising were home ownership rates, which reached
67½% in 2000, and peaked at 69% in 2004.

So while the increase in debt increasingly raised the debt ratio
of each household – one trend that culminated in the debt crisis –
it was partly associated with increased owner-occupation, which

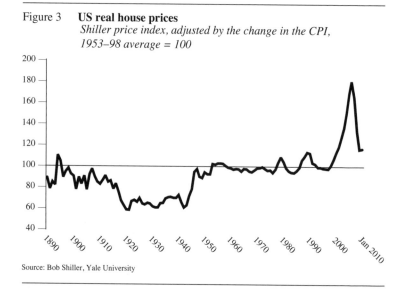

Figure 3 **US real house prices**
*Shiller price index, adjusted by the change in the CPI,
1953–98 average = 100*

Source: Bob Shiller, Yale University

tends to be regarded as a good thing. Affordability, which had
risen steadily through the 1980s to a plateau from 1993 to 2003,
started to fall back as the house-price boom took hold, and interest rates started a mild cyclical upswing from 2004. Real house
prices by 2006 were 80% higher than in 1998 and had increased
20% from 2004, despite slowing real incomes and rising rates.
Prior to this boom, real house prices had not been more than 12%
above the 1953–98 average in the previous 100 years. So it is easy
to see there was an unsustainable boom, and to date the grossly
overripe climax of it from 2004–05. But in no way does it follow
that the increase in household debt from 1980 onwards was either
avoidable or unsustainable – or undesirable.

How much must house prices fall and how much ought household debt to fall in the long deleverage now likely for US households? The good news is that house prices have completed the

bulk of the likely decline. Demand-side, affordability arguments suggest that they may already have overshot on the downside. The real price index has dropped some 35%, falling from 180% of its 1953–98 average to 115–120%.

Real house prices are still higher relative to the stable 1953–98 period than at any time over the past century. So supply-side reasoning suggests they have further to fall. And the overhang of unsold houses from the recent boom points to the same conclusion. The US construction industry is good at productivity improvements, and the country has plenty of land and natural resources to provide building materials. In principle, the cost of house-building should not rise faster than that of goods and services in general – in fact, being more of a good than a service it might be expected to share the general tendency of relative goods prices to decline vis-à-vis services, and therefore the consumer price index (CPI) *in toto*. From the point of view of long-run average costs and the current overhang of unsold properties, therefore, house prices still need to fall, perhaps by one-seventh, back to the 1953–98 average, or by more, to reflect the overhang.

Yet affordability points to a more optimistic conclusion. The low rates of interest and higher real incomes have not gone away. Neither, in all likelihood, has the appetite for more space. Affordability of housing is spectacularly higher than at any time in the past 40 years, as Figure 4 shows. Of course, this may ultimately – once the housing overhang has been worked off (at least in popular areas) – lead to more houses being built, not higher prices. But people are constrained in location by the need to get to work, see their friends, and so on. Hence the existence of cities in the first place. It is likely that such a huge gain in affordability, which owes relatively little to currently low mortgage rates as

Figure 4   **US housing affordability index**
Level of 100 means the median-income family can afford the median-priced house

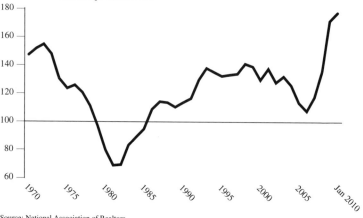

Source: National Association of Realtors

they have not come down nearly as far as money-market rates, will express itself to a degree in higher real prices, at least among the majority that live in conurbations. This suggests that the bulk of the house price decline is behind us.

It is precisely the ferocity of the house price decline that has made the debt problem worse. Estimates vary as to the proportion of mortgages that exceed the value of the homes they are financing, but numbers as high as one-half have been bandied about, though estimates of one-quarter are probably closer to the mark. Without doubt, the fall in housing values has led to a dangerous increase in the mortgage debt ratio for all US households. The total outstanding value of home mortgages is now a remarkable 62% of the total value of houses. This ratio is up from 50% as recently as the end of 2007, and 40% in 2005, illustrating the damage from the house-price crashes as well as the debt build-up (which has been negligible in the past couple of years). (Before 2005, the ratio had been stable for about ten years, with housing value gains matching the debt build-up, but not since the early 1980s has this ratio been as low as 30%.)

As large numbers of houses are owned without mortgages – that is, bought for cash or with a mortgage now paid off – the implied debt ratio for mortgaged households is clearly alarming. While some of the increase in the debt ratio may reflect mortgages that have in effect been written off, being in default or arrears, US households' balance sheets are clearly in a parlous condition. As a result, with no major revival of house prices likely in the next few years, and some chance of further declines, the rapid downward adjustment of house prices, though obviously desirable in itself, has intensified pressure for a reduction in household debt.

By how much does household debt need to fall, relative to income? The best measure seems likely to derive from the mortgage affordability concept: to assess the maximum sustainable ratio of debt service to income. The Federal Reserve Board publishes financial obligations ratios for all households, and various subgroups, including home-owning households. The data go back to 1980. These provide the best guide to what home-owners might be able to afford, and therefore by how much debt may need to be reduced.

Until 2007, the peak for interest payments by households, relative to their disposable income, was between 15% and 16% in the high leverage period of the late 1980s. However, the mortgage borrowing binge of 2005–07 increasingly featured new loans with low, 'teaser' interest rates to start with, rolling up the true interest rate into the principal, and then much higher interest rates payable later. But that 'later' of 2005–06 is now – and

Figure 5 **US home owners' debt service ratio**
Debt service + fixed financial costs as % of disposable income

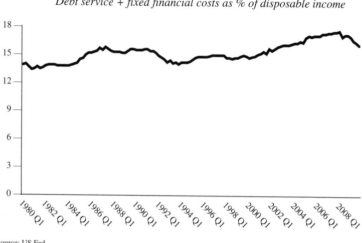

Source: US Fed

it did not show up in the debt service statistics because by the time it arrived the crisis had led to sharp falls in rates. If the new mortgages of 2005–07 had all been at their true rate to start with, the interest payments would have been much more burdensome sooner. (It was, of course, precisely to try to slip past this point that the teaser-rate system was invented.)

Interest rates were at normal (rather than currently very low) levels in 2007, though home-owners' debt service was reduced by the teaser rates. Yet debt service cost them nearly 18% of disposable income compared with what looks from Figure 5 to be a sustainable level of 14–15%. It should be remembered that large numbers of home-owners have no mortgage at all, so the burden of these payments is much higher for the rest. The natural conclusion is that US household debt needs to shift down enough to bring debt service down from 18% to below 15%, that is, by more than one-sixth. In reality, given the point about teaser rates, a cut by rather more is needed, perhaps by one-fifth. As US household debt reaches a peak of just under 100% of GDP, and household disposable income was high relative to GDP in the boom years, the rough and ready conclusion is that it needs to come down to less than 80% of GDP.

While cutting household debt from its current near 100% of GDP to less than 80% would represent a major unwinding of recent debt, it is a ratio that was first surpassed in 2002. At normal interest rates, which can be thought of as relating to 2% inflation – that is, short-term money market rates of 4% and ten-year US Treasury yields of 5% – such a debt burden would be sustainable. In no way is the US likely to return to the ratio prevailing in the 1960s and 1970s, with household debt at 45% of GDP. This conclusion is consistent with the view that the financial services revolution since the early 1980s was largely positive until about the last five years, 2003–07, of the 25-year run of that particular boom, bubble and bust.

In a pain-free world, the household debt ratio would be cut by GDP rising, not debt being reduced. But to get debt down by more than one-fifth without debt changing, GDP has to rise by more than one-quarter. The reference is to nominal GDP – hence the sudden enthusiasm of some Americans for a burst of inflation to cut the real value of the debt. But the likelihood of inflation is small; the chances of falling prices are much higher. The economy has 5–6% of slack. Unemployment of nearly 10% is far above its non-inflationary equilibrium level (see Chapter 6 for a full analysis). Moreover, higher inflation, were it to occur, would cause higher nominal interest rates, with resulting damage that would outweigh the benefit of subsequent reductions in the real debt burden. The chances of a 25% or more rise purely in real GDP is small, without waiting for ten years or so. It is unlikely debt adjustment could, should, or will be postponed that long. So household debt will have to be cut.

Debt reduction has already started in the recession. But some recovery by the end of 2009 and some residual inflation mean that nominal GDP has increased by only 0.6% since the recession started seven quarters earlier. With household debt decreasing by only 2¼% over that period, its ratio to GDP has decreased by only 3.2%, from its 96.8% peak to 93.6%. Even with modest growth from now on, it could be another 3–5 years before the ratio falls below 80%. (And if the US economy reverts to more than temporarily faster growth led by high consumer spending and little improvement in the savings rate, a rerun of the recent crisis is the most likely outcome.)

Derivatives: bankers befuddle investors (and themselves) with alphabet soup

One reason the crisis was and is as severe as it has proved is that the system had continued to churn out dubious mortgages long after the warning signals should have curtailed the business. It was perhaps too much to expect bankers, investors and borrowers to register that real house prices 80% above their previous sustainable level were hardly a sound starting point for the assumption of never-ending further increases that underlay the market's business from 2006 onwards. But it was doubling up on blind denial for the participants in this tragedy to ignore the actual and quite rapid decline in house prices that set in over the winter of 2005–06: between the autumn 2005 peak of existing home sales prices and the spring 2006 peak of the Case-Shiller index. Thus, for example, the value of US home mortgages outstanding was $8.6 trillion at the end of September 2005, rising to $10.3 trillion two years later, as the subprime crisis became evident, peaking at $10.6 trillion in March 2008. This increase of $2 trillion (23%) over two and a half years was disproportionately concentrated in subprime. Without it the crisis would have been far less acute.

The development of the alphabet soup of derivatives based on home mortgages and other loans is a classic case of something that starts as a highly original method of improving the market – creating a lot of value through lowering the cost of capital – matures into a highly efficient and major portion of the overall market, and then blows itself out in an orgy of excess. The structure and rationale for mortgage-backed securities (MBSs), collateralised debt obligations (CDOs) and further developments of the alphabet soup are described in Appendix 1.

The 20% upsurge of real house prices between 2004 and their peak in 2006, and the corresponding late-boom surge of mortgage creation, also illustrate how the worst features of the housing bubble were concentrated in a relatively short spike at the end of it. This is typical of bubbles. It is the mirror image of the capitulation at the end of a panic and crash. Capitulation consists of resistance finally collapsing. In the case of a crash, the last of the bulls throws in the towel and joins the panic. In the reverse case of an end-bubble spike, it is the sceptics, the bears, whose resistance finally collapses, and they rush to join in the last stages of the upswing.

In September 2004, when I published the Monthly Review for Lombard Street Research that was the first exposition of the savings-glut idea, it was widely anticipated that the US would have a problem financing its current-account deficit. But that review pointed out the role of the savers, the surplus countries, in global imbalances (see page 42), meaning the US would have no such problem. Instead it argued that a continuation of the trend would ensure a household debt crisis in due course. If Bernanke, then moving towards a similar conclusion, had taken clear action to check housing excesses when house prices peaked, some of the subsequent grief might have been avoided. However, to have done so, he would have had to ignore violent objections from monetarists, Keynesians, all political parties and most journals, not to mention the unemployed, who would have seen policy restraint as unnecessary, given that growth was reasonable, not excessive, and inflation low.

Two important conclusions follow. First, using hindsight to place heavy blame on policymakers or even bankers is unreasonable, as they would have had to defy the overwhelming balance of conventional wisdom (and competitive pressure, in the bankers' case) to have prevented the housing bubble. Second, as Appendix 1 makes clear, much of what was done in creating the alphabet soup of derivatives had legitimate origins in improved capital market functioning. The late-stage deception, rating agency behaviour, and the general complexity and opacity of some of the derivatives created became rapidly more culpable in 2004–07. But with proper regulation and transparency the financial innovations should be allowed to revive and perform their function of improving the allocation and reducing the cost of capital.

Business debt: bubbles in 1989, 1999 and 2007

Business debt as much as household mortgages was a focus of constant financial sector innovation from the early 1980s. While the household debt ratio rose consistently, however, only pausing between booms (for example, in the early 1990s), the non-financial business debt ratio went through three separate surges, with a distinct fallback between each. In other words, it has been, and is likely to remain, far more cyclical. The underlying boom periods that took the ratio up to new peaks each time, vis-à-vis GDP, were high leverage culminating in 1989, the stockmarket bubble that blew out from 2000 onward, and then the private-equity-led leveraged buy-out (LBO) surge at the end of the recent debt bubble in 2007. As to the resulting vulnerability of non-financial business balance sheets, and finances in general, the 1999–2000 debt build-up was clearly the most threatening, the 1989 boom being at lower debt ratios, and the 2007 boom occurring at a time of much stronger business profitability and cash flow.

Financial sector debt is another matter: its ratio to GDP soared throughout the 25 years we are considering from around 20% of GDP in 1980 to nearly 120% at the peak in late 2008. But this can be separated from the discussion here of non-financial business debt, and is better considered as part of the analysis of the Wall Street boom that was an integral part of the symbiosis of borrowers, intermediaries and lenders contributing to the particular virulence of the crisis (see Chapter 3 for the crisis and Appendix 1 for the development of the alphabet soup). So here the focus will be on levels of non-financial business debt, not the elaborate proliferation of swaps and other derivatives that facilitated the adoption of greater debt leverage.

After the huge profitable boom of the 1960s, US business lapsed into bureaucratic and often conglomerated sloth in the 1970s, with a sharp decline in productivity growth. Value added reached post-war lows relative to operating assets employed. Gross trading profit (earnings before interest, tax and depreciation or EBITDA) reached lows even relative to this weak output performance. Shareholder value was the goal that underpinned the emergence from this slough. Debt was a key instrument – better in quality owing to the financial innovations, and greater in quantity to reflect both the spreading of risk, but, more importantly, the need to put pressure on corporate managements to serve shareholder interests, not softly defined stakeholder interests that were little more than cover for bureaucracy and empire-building.

Crucial to the sharpening of American business with extra debt was the development of 'junk' bonds by Mike Milken of Drexel Burnham Lambert, and their use in a wave of predatory, hostile takeovers by 'policemen of capitalism' such as T. Boone Pickens and Carl Icahn. A classic case was the assault on Gulf Oil in 1984. Pickens launched a bid that would leverage Gulf 'up to the eyeballs' with debt that would be syndicated by Milken. After the usual ups and downs, the Big Oil wagons circled to repel the assault, and Socal drew the short straw, taking over Gulf. To outbid Pickens, the combined entity (named Chevron) was necessarily loaded up with debt.

Viewed economically, the principal value of the extra debt was that it stopped Gulf (and then Chevron) engaging in Big Oil's favourite pastime – exploring for fresh sources of oil. Pickens's insight was that Gulf had (much) more value with no exploration expense than it had with exploration expense. In other words, the net present value of fresh oil discoveries was (heavily) negative. By 1984, oil prices, which had peaked in the second oil crisis of 1979–80, had fallen by nearly half in real terms from their peak. The world was economising on oil usage, and previous high prices had induced plenty of new discoveries. At then prices, exploration was uneconomic. After falling more up to mid-1985, crude oil prices halved again in just one year, from mid-1985 to mid-1986. So Pickens saved Big Oil from huge losses in exploration expense. Heavily leveraging relative stable downstream activities with debt forced the companies to attend to shareholder value rather than the bureaucratic priority of size, and the macho exploration habit.

While the Milken-led takeover boom blew itself out from 1989 onwards, with Milken and Drexel barred from the securities industries fold by concerted Wall Street action (denial of credit lines) in 1990, the benefits of extra non-financial business debt continued. The emblematic takeover based on this approach was RJR Nabisco in 1988. No stream of business cash flows is steadier than tobacco sales, and few more than food processing. This was the obvious company to leverage equity returns by raising the lower-cost debt ratio in its balance sheet. The hard-fought takeover battle raised the ultimate private-equity takeover price considerably, and ensured that the greatest pressure was put on future management to cut costs to the minimum. A follow-up private leveraged bid for British America Tobacco in 1989 was beaten off by management, but only by taking on a huge mountain of debt. As a result, BAT had to stop using its cash flow for the fatuous series of diversifications it had been pursuing for the previous 20–30 years.

By putting pressure on management to focus on profits, and to cut out waste, the leveraged takeover threat helped boost productivity growth in the US, and later Britain. This was the foundation of the shareholder value concept that has dominated managements over the past couple of decades. Hostile takeovers were the weapon of choice in the 1980s, but from the 1990s onwards, private equity, often using the skills of existing management, was

Figure 6   **US growth in output/worker-hour**
           % per year

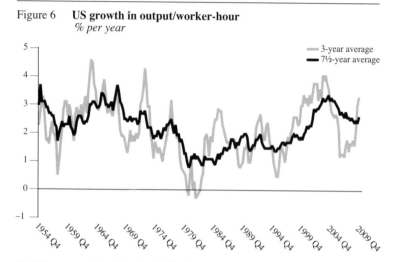

Note: 7½-year average is largely free of cyclical effect, 3-year average gives recent cyclical change.
Source: US Bureau of Labor Statistics

the normal bidder. Hostile takeovers suffer from the inevitable disadvantage that the seller (generally the existing management) knows more about the assets than an outside buyer. On average, public market corporate takeovers have destroyed value for the shareholders of the acquiring company. The 1980s provided a particular opportunity in the form of bloated targets, with sleepy managements, and a bold new instrument, the junk bond. This provided a degree of risk between that of traditional, investment-grade debt and equity, but with the tax deductibility of debt interest, in contrast to the need to pay dividends out of after-tax profits. But in general, once obvious stockmarket undervaluation from 1974 to 1982 had been eliminated, the private-equity approach was bound to work better – as the RJR Nabisco deal made clear.

By the time of Milken's disgrace and the bankruptcy of Drexel in 1990, the junk-bond market was a widespread phenomenon, engaged in by mainstream banks and businesses. The power of the takeover threat generated shareholder value no longer through the mergers themselves so much as the threat of them. In the recession and jobless recovery of 1990–93, US business implemented a wave of restructuring that started a major upswing of productivity growth trends – whether measured as output per worker-hour or total factor productivity. (The former measure includes in productivity growth the effect of extra capital employed. The latter is what is left of output gains after stripping out both employment gains and extra capital employed. As such it is the best measure of pure productivity, though difficult to measure and to explain.) It would be wrong to attribute all the improvement of US productivity growth since the 1980s to extra debt leverage. But the combination of pressure on management resulting from having to service a high debt load, and fear resulting from the potential use of debt to finance a takeover bid, was a major causative factor.

The capacity of debt to reinforce folly, rather than just motivate tough cost control and productivity gains, was shown in the next round of business debt build-up, this time as part of the stockmarket bubble of the late 1990s. The driving force was hysteria over stock prices, led by the tech-stocks but by no means confined to them. The stockmarket soared and took price/book-value ratios to ludicrous heights. Whereas the average stock price ratio to accounting book value in US non-financial companies has been 75% over the past 50–60 years, it spiked up to a peak of 180% in March 2000. (Its peak in the 1960s boom was only just over 100%.) With the price/book ratio much higher in many sectors, it became highly profitable to float companies on the stock exchange. People could borrow money to finance assets that were then saleable at a huge profit in the stockmarket. Debt-financed

Figure 7   **US non-financial companies' debt ratio**

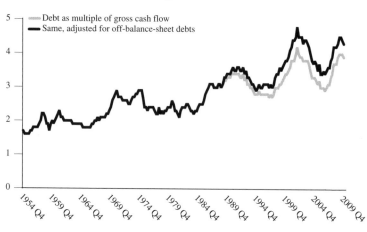

Sources: US Fed; BEA

capital spending soared and transformed the stockmarket bubble into an overload of business-sector debt and excess capacity – leading to the (mild, investment-led) recession of 2001.

The combination of excess debt and capacity in 1997–2000 undermined profits from 1998 onwards. So the ratio of debt to gross cash flow was doubly raised: debt was up and cash flow down. The investment-led recession of 2001 was followed by continued action by business to repay debt and improve cash flow for several years. Non-financial companies' debt fell relative to gross cash flow until mid-2006. For the three years to mid-2004, debt itself was level and cash flow improving. For the next two years, in which growth was strong, debt started to rise significantly, but cash flow outpaced it.

Mid-2006 was, as we have seen, the point at which the upswing of household debt should have stopped – as house prices started their long decline – but did not. So the last 12–18 month surge of private debt was a two-engine affair with seriously misallocated subprime mortgages being supplemented by soaring non-financial business debt, mostly to finance private-equity buyouts. However, the company debt/cash-flow ratio did not rise as high as in 2000–01. And its increase was almost entirely used to finance stock buybacks and buy-outs, not fixed investment. Luckily for US companies, the subprime crisis struck before corporate debt became crippling. It was possible to stop debt rising quickly – by simply ending buy-outs and buybacks. At the same time, US business reverted to its cost-cutting fever of 1991–93 and 2001–05. This accelerated the recession in 2008–09, but left gross cash flow, and especially its surplus over capital spending, also slashed, reasonably strong.

The story of the recession is told below (see Chapter 3) – here we are concerned with the sustainable level of business debt. The total of non-financial business debt is nearly half as much again as corporate debt, owing to the large unincorporated business sector, both farm and non-farm. It may be that unincorporated businesses are more stretched than companies. But allowing for gross cash flow being harmed by the recession, though nowhere near as badly as in 2000–01, and the need to bring the debt ratio to it down by perhaps 15–20%, a ratio of 70–75% of GDP looks sustainable. This is below the recent 81%. But that is itself down in less than a year from its peak of 85%: the decline needed to reach 70–75% looks like a cyclical shift rather than the major structural reduction required by household debt. The chief need is for some of the more aggressive late-boom private-equity buyouts to rebalance their balance sheets with asset sales, equity boosts and a few years' cash flow. This means that debt deflation is not threatened by business-sector behaviour of the sort that plagued Japan from 1997 to 2002, especially given a broad and deep stockmarket to recapitalise extreme cases.

The potential for a large debt load to stimulate effective business conduct in America should come as no surprise to students of the post-second-world-war recoveries in Germany and Japan. The German *Wirtschaftswunder* in the 1950s and 1960s, and the super-rapid catch-up growth about five years behind this in Japan, focused on the *zaibatsu* system of bank-centred industrial conglomerations, both featured high debt loads in business as part of their motivating force – and to great effect in their heyday. Nor was the eventual drastic slowdown in each case a function of too much debt, though Japan's boom did indeed blow itself out in a bubble in 1988–90. The slow growth in both these countries in recent years can in no way be attributed to excessive levels of business debt. It is bound up with the inability of both countries to want, plan for and develop a fully functional domestic consumer-based economy. In both cases, the fear is that working-age population decline will mean future income is inadequate to fund pension commitments to increased numbers of retired people. These fears have fed into policies and behaviour that have had the paradoxical effect of reducing income growth and in effect making those fears self-fulfilling in the present.

The Eurasian savings glut, starting in 1998

For every borrower there is a lender. For every deficit there is a surplus. The sum of financial flows in the economy, any economy, is nil. While the world as a whole is a closed economy, individual

Figure 8   **Eurasian current-account surpluses**
$ billion

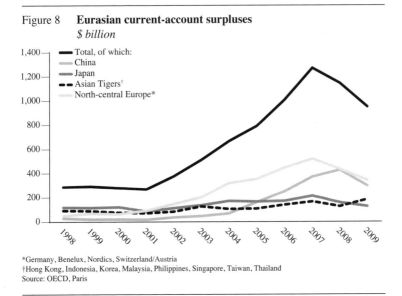

*Germany, Benelux, Nordics, Switzerland/Austria
†Hong Kong, Indonesia, Korea, Malaysia, Philippines, Singapore, Taiwan, Thailand
Source: OECD, Paris

countries are not. We are accustomed to see deficits (borrowing) as the action, and the equal and opposite surpluses (lending) as the reaction. This is true both between open economies in the world at large, and within economies (closed or open) between borrowers and lenders. But it is no more than custom. The Eurasian savings glut, shown in balance-of-payments terms in Figure 8, is an independently determined phenomenon – an action – that has not arisen in response to developments elsewhere in the world. After looking at the nature of the glut, it will be interesting to see to what extent it caused US and other countries' policy to be so easy in 2002–06, leading to the run-up of debt that ensured crisis.

The Eurasian savings glut has different causes in different Eurasian countries. Broadly, in the advanced economies, Japan and Germany and surrounding countries (north-central Europe, or NCE), the glut is partly demographic – the result of actual and impending population decline – and partly an effect of business restructuring. As such it is at root a private-sector financial surplus – a desire to save that hugely exceeds the need to invest. In the developing Pacific-Asian economies, China and the Asian Tigers, public policy plays a larger role. To be sure, the fairly backward financial systems in China and most of the Tigers mean that private saving is higher than it might be with more sophisticated financial products and greater social security. But a mercantilist emphasis on export-led growth is a major part of the drive towards surplus, as we shall see. So for the advanced economies the private sector's net financial balance is the best measure of a tendency to savings glut, while for the developing economies the current-account balance is the better measure.

These assertions refer only to the structural surpluses of the Eurasian glut countries. As well as the structure of behaviour and policy, this includes secular phenomena such as the demographics of the baby-boomers that involve high (late-career) saving now and the likelihood of low saving as that population cohort gradually passes into retirement. Oil exporters are excluded, as their surpluses, when they have them, are not structural, but cyclical – quickly eliminated when cyclical downswings of oil prices occur (often in tandem with delayed-reaction upswings in oil exporters' spending and imports). The same is true of commodity-dependent developing countries in general. The savings-glut countries, by contrast, are in surplus because of deep-seated policy and behaviour. Their appetite for surplus has proved largely impervious to the 'price' of money – that is, the real rate of interest – or the return on capital. While real and nominal interest rates have dived in the current recession, the current-account surplus of savings-glut countries fell (see Figure 8) for other reasons: their

Figure 9   **Real bond yields before the crisis, %**

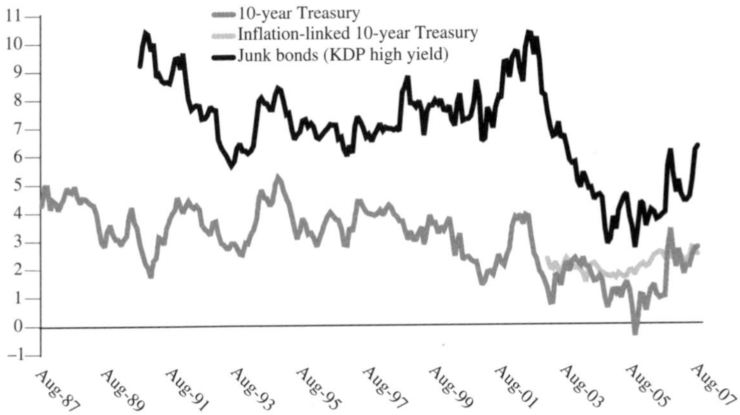

Sources: US Fed; BLS; KDP; Datastream

economies were export-led, so when deficit countries slashed borrow-and-spend, their trade surpluses naturally fell.

The point about the price of money – the real rate of interest, the credit-spread for private-sector borrowers – is fundamental. After the event, the volume of borrowing necessarily has equalled the volume of lending. When it comes to intentions before the event, excess demand to borrow vis-à-vis desire to save drives up real interest rates. Excess desire to save vis-à-vis demand for loans drives them down. So the movement of real interest rates indicates which is the driver and which the driven. If a large increase in turnover in any market coincides with a falling price, it is necessarily supply driven; for example, a bumper apple harvest drives down prices to ensure the extra apples are sold. If higher turnover coincides with a rising price, it is necessarily demand-driven. Under this logic, Figure 9 shows a sustained downward trend in real rates until 2006, with the upswing in 2001 reflecting purely the temporary dip of the denominator, inflation, caused by recession. So the key period of increasing capital market and imbalance build-up, from the bubble-bust in 2001 to early 2006, saw falling real interest rates, a lower price of money. Supply of capital, excess saving vis-à-vis appetite for investment, was therefore the driving force in the expansion of activity during this period. It was only in the climax of 2006–07 that US profligacy took over the lead role.

Asia's decisive shift into current-account surplus was after the 1997–98 Asian crisis. Before that, structural surpluses were largely confined to Japan, and in global terms were small. For China and the Asian Tigers, the mercantilist urge towards export-led growth was a prime cause of their glut of savings. Export-led growth has in any case been the preferred policy for Pacific-Asian countries since Japan started down this road in the 1950s, followed by South Korea in the 1970s. And it has worked far better than the old-style development economics, emphasising supply to the domestic market, and import substitution, as followed in Latin America, and India until the 1980s. But the Asian crisis of 1997–98 saw countries in financial difficulties mercilessly punished by the IMF and other institutions, representing (at one remove) the interests of western governments and international banks. China and the Tigers emerged from that experience with iron determination to avoid such humiliation in future. The urge towards export-led growth was heavily boosted.

Initially from 1998, the Asian Tiger surpluses, flowing from countries traumatised by crisis, strongly reinforced the Wall Street bubble of 1998–2000; then they drove the British and Australian debt-fuelled housing booms of 1999–2004. These countries developed large, easily financed deficits during this period. American households followed suit from late 2001, and Asian surpluses were recycled back into a Chinese domestic investment boom in 2002–04. To this private-sector debt stimulation must be added acceptance in the United States, Europe and Japan of government deficits that were and are far beyond what is generally regarded as prudent – especially in the context of looming baby-boomers' pension financing problems in most of these countries.

Layered onto the long-standing Japanese savings glut, and that of the Tigers from 1998–99 onwards, were German-centred NCE surpluses from 2002 and export-led growth in China from 2005. The NCE surpluses sprang from a similar source to Japan's. Actual and potential declines in population – total and of working age – lowered the need for investment, especially in construction. The predominant baby-boomer generation, in mid to late career – the high-saving period of a typical life cycle – and fearing an under-funded retirement, boosted the aggregate household savings rate. In this context, lower real returns to capital, and lower real interest rates, act perversely on behaviour. As the cumulative return on saving is lower, the rate of saving has to increase (in response to the lower price of money) in order to provide the target level of future income. Layered onto this structural widening of the margin of saving over investment came the restructuring of NCE businesses from 2002 onwards, in an attempt to catch up with American standards of capital productivity. Capital spending and inventories were more strictly controlled, and cost cutting helped raise business cash flow – both trends contributing to greater net saving.

China now has the largest individual country's current-account surplus. (Japan probably exceeds China in pure, private-sector savings glut, but absorbs most of it with government deficits.) China had very little surplus as recently as 2004. But the rapid growth of exports had started earlier, merely being offset until 2004 by an overheated domestic investment boom. When that had to be cooled off, and growth in the domestic economy sharply reduced (from mid-2004), continued ultra-rapid (typically 30% a year) export growth caused the trade and current-account surpluses to soar, with an extra boost as the import content of exports eased down from around 50% to around 40%. The current-account surplus rose from $69 billion in 2004 to $372 billion in 2007, and reached $426 billion in 2008, only kept down to that level by the export-led collapse at the end of the year. China's savings glut certainly involves high private savings as a result of the relatively limited financial options available to its citizens, but a primary force is the mercantilist drive for exports (see Chapter 6 for an analysis of China's economy).

By 2007, the savings glut had reached $1,270 billion, measured in current-account terms (as in Figure 9) and a little more, $1,300 billion, if measured by adding China and Asian Tiger current-account balances to Japanese and NCE private-sector financial surpluses. With world GDP at $55 trillion in 2007, these sums were about 2¼%. But the GDP of the countries concerned, advanced countries plus China and the Asian Tigers, is probably the better point of comparison, and was $44 trillion, making the savings glut 3% of it. For the savings-glut countries themselves, the surplus averaged 7¾% of GDP, breaking down to 6½% for NCE, 11% for China, 6% for the Tigers and 7½% for Japan.

The Eurasian countries' surpluses in 1998 were heavily concentrated in Japan. Over the next nine years, the surplus shifted strongly away from Japan, the countervailing government deficits were reversed to surplus in NCE and much reduced in Japan, and the growth of China's surplus, combined with meteoric GDP growth, led the glut to mount rapidly, as a percentage of world GDP as well as in dollar terms. For the future this means the source and development of the glut must be analysed strictly in relation to the relevant economies: it is not some 'bloc' phenomenon in its origins, only in its effects on other countries (money in a globalised world being largely fungible). (For those interested in how the savings glut came about, and its economic effects, Appendix 2 has more details.)

A private-sector savings glut in any country represents a deficiency of demand relative to potential supply/income. The ways it can express itself are thus limited to:

- a net export surplus – the deficiency of demand is made up by foreigners buying goods and services and running a trade/current-account deficit;
- wasteful investment – if interest rates become negligible, or the flush of cash induces carelessness, wasteful investment may use up, or more precisely cancel, some of the excess savings;
- structural government deficits – the government may run consistent, medium-term current- or capital-account deficits to create excess demand and offset the private-sector deficiency;
- output and income collapse, leading to cyclical government deficits – if none of above occurs, demand will be inadequate and output and income will collapse, reducing savings anyhow, and causing a recessionary, cyclical government deficit that offsets such excess saving as persists.

The economics of the responses to the Eurasian savings glut

prior to the 2007–09 crisis are analysed in Appendix 2. The possibility of reduced saving in glut countries is considered there, but will be excluded here, because the chief conclusion is the one described above (page 47) – lower real interest rates tend, if anything, to raise saving, especially in households. (To the extent savings were lowered by easy money, this was mostly in other countries, notably the US, but this comes under the effects of the glut on the rest of the world, discussed below, not the effect within savings-glut countries, the topic here. Such international effects are covered in some detail in Appendix 2, which is the main discussion of the controversial events of 2002–06, the period dominated by Fed chairman Alan Greenspan.) Lower real rates may, of course, also raise investment, probably by more than they cause households to save more, and that is covered under the second and third points above.

The chief, the 'nice', outlet for a savings glut, of course, is other countries' readiness to run a deficit equal to the structural savings glut. This was more or less what happened in 2002–07, as the US and other deficit countries ran up their domestic debt levels. But, as forecast by some of us at the time, this was unsustainable. So the discussion moves on to what sort of policies savings-glut countries might adopt as and when the US and other deficit countries cease their borrowing. The analysis of how that borrowing has switched to the public sector, while the private sector in the deficit nations has moved into surplus, and how the world economy may develop as a result, is reserved for Chapter 4. Here we need to consider how the limited outlets for a savings glut crystallised in their massive recessions, worse, in the event, for China, Japan and Germany than the US and Britain.

Option two, excessive investment, has been adopted by that

savings-glut veteran, Japan, in both the private and the public sector. The public-sector aspect of this – the famous 'bridges to nowhere', 'vegetable airports', 'paving Mount Fuji', and so on – overlaps with option three, structural government deficits. But even in the private sector the investment rate has been high, despite 20 years of weak growth suggesting little need for new capacity or equipment. Thus gross business investment averaged some 15% of GDP over the 12 years to 2008, with a slightly rising curve in the last few years. By contrast, in the US, where average real GDP growth has been 2–3 times Japan's nugatory 1%, business investment averaged 11½% of GDP over the same period. Japan's rate of business investment has to be regarded as wasteful. Much the same may be true in China, at a much higher percentage of GDP and real growth, and this is discussed in Chapter 5. In Germany and the NCE generally, the private sector has been more rigorous in its use of capital.

The contrast between Japan and Germany carries over to option three, structural government deficits. These are standard in Japan and anathema in Germany. The Japanese government likes neither its deficits nor the resultant government debt of 100% of GDP (net), 200% (gross). But it has opted for them as an alternative to economic collapse (see option four above) since the mid-1990s. In the brutal 1998 recession, the Japanese government deficit reached 12% of GDP. It then remained at the 7–8% level for the five years 1999–2003, which contained another whole recession. During those five years the private sector's net surplus averaged 10% of GDP (even after the wasteful business investment). So the current deficit was only 2½% of GDP, reflecting one-quarter of Japan's savings glut, the other three-quarters being absorbed by government deficit. In 2004–07 the Japanese government cut its deficit hard to around 2½% of GDP. But in the process its dependence mounted on export-led growth and American willingness to take on debt. As a result it suffered the worst major country recession in the recent crisis. Its structural government deficit is back up to the 7% region. Such is the relentless impact of a savings glut.

To say the savings-glut countries chose option four, output and income collapse, is too bitter. But by refusing the domestic alternatives and blindly assuming they could all enjoy export-led growth – while smugly criticising the debt and deficits of the countries whose borrowing and imports provided them with an income – they effectively made that choice. A collapse of exports was, of course, the mechanism by which their output and income was hammered. The collapse ran for six months between November 2008 and April 2009. It was aggravated by the deficit countries' recessions provoking a major downswing in the global inventory cycle, so that output had to fall much faster even than final demand. In volume terms (that is, excluding price changes) exports fell by one-third in China at the worst, by two-fifths in Japan and by one-quarter in Germany. As exports respectively represent about 40%, 17% and 50% of GDP, the resulting recessions were brutal. Japan had an 8½% recession (from peak to trough), China 7% (on my calculations) and Germany 6½%. To the surprise of people who did not understand the fundamental role of the savings glut in the financial crisis, these recessions were worse than the US (4%) or even Britain (6%).

US deficits, while partly driven by the entrenched habit of borrowing, are in part the reaction to structural Eurasian surpluses, and at times entirely. Profligate extravagance came into play in 1998–2000, and again in 2006–07, as we have seen. But the

2001–05 deficits and borrowing that bridged these two periods – and entrenched the habit of borrowing to deal with problems – was simply the result of pursuing full-employment/low-inflation policies in a world full of countries determined to run surpluses. This is not an iron-clad, bullet-proof assertion. Elements of fiscal and monetary irresponsibility can be found in US policies, but the broad direction of causation is clear. Asian (and some European) countries run high-savings/current-account surplus economies partly as a matter of policy and partly for deep structural and behavioural reasons. America and to a lesser degree Britain, Australia and European countries such as Spain, Greece and Ireland simply adjusted their fiscal and monetary policies to use Asia's excess savings. It would have been rude to refuse. More to the point, if the borrowers had not willingly run deficits on a large and increasing scale in 2001–05, the world economy would not have recovered from the stockmarket bubble's bursting in 2000–02.

In this interpretation of recent events, the one problem that has long ceased to exist is the US trade or current-account deficit. The problem has not for a dozen years at least been for the United States to fund its deficit. Rather, the problem is for the Asian, together with some European, countries to find a home for the capital generated by their surpluses. This surplus has moved like a tidal wave from balance sheet to balance sheet, between businesses, households and government, loading them up with extra debt. It has helped induce undue borrowing by US business (1998–2000), by Australian and British households, by American households (2001–2008), by the world's private-equity moguls in leveraged buy-outs (2006–07) and progressively by Spain, Greece, Portugal and Ireland around Europe's periphery.

The profound destructiveness of the Eurasian savings glut is vigorously denied in China and Germany, though hapless Japan understands it while remaining by now virtually powerless to remedy the entrenched domestic imbalances and deflation. The Chinese economy is discussed in some detail in Chapter 5. Here we can observe that after a violent domestic stimulus in the winter of 2008–09, when China was the country with the liveliest response to the crisis, the country benefited from rapid gains in export competitiveness through its yuan-dollar peg, and has now slipped back to export-led growth. This time, the gains are as much at the expense of other exporters, not advancing in a general world trade boom, as was mostly the case in 2005–08. In Germany, a constitutional amendment has just been passed – requiring an impossible two-thirds majority in both the Bundestag and Bundesrat to be repealed – mandating virtually nil structural budget deficits for ever. This fits with the country's fanatical devotion to budget balance and moralistic rejection of debt. As the private sector is unlikely to lessen its structural surplus for a long time, the danger is a severe deflation of output and prices, centred on Germany, but rippling out over the whole of Europe and reinforcing the recession in Mediterranean Europe as those countries attempt to reduce their deficits.

Fixed exchange rates: savings gluttons beggar their neighbours

Yuan-dollar peg and the New Dollar Area
China pegged its yuan to the dollar in 1994 in good faith as a stabilising measure after the major 1994 devaluation. This followed loss of monetary control and 30% inflation in 1993. Ironically,

the yuan-dollar peg has been a major destabilising force, at least since 2001. In effect, it weakened the needed adjustment of exchange rates with dollar decline from early 2002. The dollar, unlike sterling, cannot float freely if other countries insist on pegging their currencies to it, in its role as the world's reserve currency. After private capital flows into the dollar dried up in early 2002, it should have been possible for it to depreciate to the level at which investors recovered their appetite, probably with higher bond yields as part of the bargain. This might or might not have involved improvement in the US current deficit, or perhaps lessening of some of the Eurasian surpluses. But it would have balanced out the financing of such imbalances with the cost-benefit analysis of investors providing the counterpart capital flows.

The drastic cuts in US short-term interest rates in 2001–03 were at least partly intended to achieve this prophylactic decline in the dollar. Because of the yuan-dollar peg, it did not happen – or rather it happened in the wrong way. The dollar went down, but mostly against European currencies, as well as its major North American trading partners, Canada and Mexico. China's fixed yuan rate (until July 2005) meant its real effective exchange rate went down too. The Japanese yen, which was to some extent shadowing the yuan – Japan was terrified of its manufacturing industry being hollowed out by China – also declined. But of course, the ultra-competitiveness was in Asia, not Europe. The dollar needed to go down against the Asian currencies – when in fact all that was achieved was devaluation against the competition that did not matter so much.

Figure 10 shows that China's real exchange rate was relatively steady at 70–80 from 1990 to 2006, excluding the brief spell of inflation and devaluation in 1993–94. Clearly the '100'

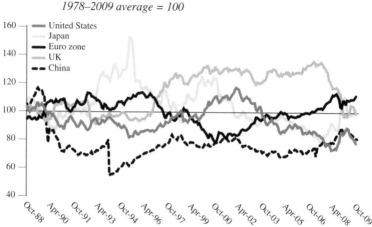

Figure 10   **Real effective exchange rates**
1978–2009 average = 100

Note: Based on relative normalised unit labour costs, except China which is relative price based.
Source: IMF

level relates to the gross overvaluation in the 1980s, which is irrelevant. But the right rate for the yuan in the 1990s is hardly right now. Between the yuan peg's establishment in 1994 and now, China has made a quantum leap in global economic significance. It is the dominant economy regionally, given its far greater participation in foreign trade than Japan. The yuan peg gave support to the Pacific region during the gross upheavals of the Asian Crisis in 1997–98. But the increased size of China, and its huge advantage in cost competitiveness, has been an increasing concern for Asian countries from Japan downwards. Over the past 15–20 years they have been hollowed out by China's takeover of much of the world's manufacturing.

The combination of the yuan peg with the dollar's decline from early 2002 confronted Asian competitors with the risk of even greater Chinese cost competitiveness. Their response was what we at Lombard Street Research (following Brian Reading) called the New Dollar Area (NDA) – a semi-fixed-rate currency zone including China, Japan and the Asian Tigers, bound together by the mortar of fear, China-fear. Japan and those Asian Tigers without existing dollar pegs managed their exchange rates by intervention to ensure they stayed competitive – not with the dollar, US competition being no problem, but with China and its yuan.

As a result, the more than 20% cut in the real exchange rate of the US between early 2002 and 2005–06 (that is, the improvement in its global cost competitiveness with trading partners) led to a 10% cut in that of the real yuan, to China's cost advantage, and in that of the Japanese yen, together with much of the rest of the Pacific rim countries. The bulk of the Eurasian structural surpluses corresponding to the US deficit lies in the Pacific rim, with which the US made no gain in cost competitiveness. (Although north-central Europe was part of the savings glut, most of its counterpart deficit was in Europe.) Asian countries had their costs heavily trimmed vis-à-vis Europe's, and the market share gains within Europe that resulted were achieved much more by Asian exporters than by American ones. In the US market itself, Asians were enabled to gain share from Europeans faster than would have occurred in any case. With the Asian/US competitiveness locked in place, expansion in the US raised its imports and ensured no deficit reduction took place. The US current deficit, 4% of GDP in 2000–01, rose to 6% of GDP in 2006, despite devaluation. Some adjustment!

In July 2005, China relaxed its fixed rate for the yuan of 8.28 per dollar in favour of a managed appreciation. In the event, the rate reached around 6.83 in July 2008, up 21% from June 2005, since when it has been fixed again. This 21% appreciation was only against the dollar, and fell into two phases. For the first 27 months, to October 2007, the shift was just over 10%, from 8.28 to just over 7.50, less than 5% a year. Then the evident global financial crisis led China to accelerate the appreciation to reach 6.83 within nine more months, that is, a further 10%. In the first phase, the real appreciation started as negligible, partly because of dollar weakness. The real effective yuan (based on relative CPIs) was unchanged for the first 21 months after the appreciation started, though by October 2007 it was up about 10%. By July 2008, when the rate was (informally) re-fixed at 6.83, the real effective rate was up another 6½%, significantly less than the extra 10% appreciation against the dollar. Since then the real yuan exchange rate has gone up and then down again with the dollar, and remains at the top end of the 15% trading range (roughly 70–80 in Figure 10) that has prevailed since 1990.

How does China now compare with the China of 1990? Its GDP has averaged 10% real growth over 20 years, increasing from 1.7% to 8.3% of world GDP, measured at current prices and exchange rates, and from 3.6% to 12.5% at purchasing-power parity. Its exports were a smaller share of the world's than its GDP in 1990, at 1.3%, but were 8.8% of world exports in 2009. Even with the 2009 export recession of 16%, their growth over 20 years was 30 times (in dollars) compared with 3.8 times for world exports of goods and services. The Chinese increase has less inflation in it than the world total, so the contrast in real growth is even greater. The exchange rate that has permitted these gains in world market share can only get more disruptive as that share becomes an ever more important part of the world total. Holding onto this exchange rate in such conditions is clear, beggar-thy-neighbour mercantilism.

EMU fosters European imbalances

In Europe, as in the trans-Pacific US/Pacific-Asian imbalances, fixed exchange rates are a key factor. The comparable imbalances within Europe were encouraged and have been made more damaging by fixed rates in EMU (Economic and Monetary Union). EMU inevitably encourages imbalances. The very concept of convergence of income – a major goal of EMU – requires divergence of growth and (almost certainly) inflation. Thus Spain, still backward in the 1990s, should catch up with the core euro-zone countries (Germany, Benelux and France) through faster growth and inflation. The EMU structure removes the previous constraint on Spain that its faster growth and inflation would lead to higher interest rates (than in the core) and thus slow down its catch-up. Likewise, EMU interest rates, being set to meet conditions in the whole euro zone, are higher than would otherwise prevail in the lower-growth, low-inflation core. So core countries are slowed by EMU. The exaggeration of growth and inflation in Spain, and the curbing of them in the core, widened financial imbalances dramatically.

Similarly, on the exchange-rate front, imbalances that arise from excessive wages or deficiencies of industrial structure lead to imbalances in trade that do not have to be corrected, as the deficits can be financed under the general umbrella of the euro. Thus Italy's grotesque uncompetitiveness in costs and products has not led to enforced discipline, as the external world has financed Italian deficits without noticing them – as would certainly not be the case were Italy not protected by the much-vaunted financial stability arising from EMU membership. Put another way, financial instability is not always bad, but rather a useful advance warning that something is wrong with economic fundamentals. A

Figure 11   **Real effective exchange rates: major European economies**
1978–2009 average = 100

Note: Based on relative normalised unit labour costs.
Source: IMF

dachshund with a bad back, given painkillers, repeats the actions that injured its back, and thus destroys itself.

EMU's painkiller effect is waning fast, and its malignant economic effects are waxing to match. Stuck within EMU, Italy cannot restore competitiveness except through even greater falls in real income than its feeble supply-side performance makes necessary in any case. Germany's competitiveness may have been enhanced by EMU, but that will lose value if its significant Mediterranean export markets are in long-run decline. In these conditions, the structural weakness of German domestic demand is reinforced by poor exports, so that a downward spiral sets in. Of course, growth in third markets will soften the impact of this unhealthy embrace. But weakness and more competitive exchange rates in the US and Britain, as well as other major European economies and central-eastern Europe (facing prolonged structural adjustment), make this cold comfort.

In the trans-Pacific economy and within EMU, fixed exchange rates have been a crucial factor in building up imbalances. In both instances, the borrowing end of the imbalances hit crisis first, yet the recession has been worse for the lending, export-led party. Yet both China and Germany cling to their fixed-rate systems, even though it is clear that the post-crisis world will not permit them to enjoy the advantages they had in 2002–07. The future of these fixed rates will be a key part of the discussion of world prospects later in this book (see Chapter 10).

Blame: bankers, rating agencies, regulators, investors

Reviewing these factors separately, the impossibility of blaming one particular cause, person, or group of people for the crisis is clear. But that does not rule out conclusions about how the crisis fomented. The answer seems to be a nexus of blame involving mortgage brokers, bankers, rating agencies, regulators and investors. This is on the assumption that we exclude the irresponsible borrowers who accepted mortgage money to buy houses knowing that the loans they were committing to were beyond their means. This exclusion is a stretch, but can be justified by reference to the widespread assumption that house prices would continue to rise, and that 'teaser' mortgage structures would create space for some form of clean exit from the initial mortgage.

Also largely excluded from direct blame must be US monetary policy, and the surplus policies of savings-glut countries. It is fun to make jokes about Greenspan's bubble-blowing tendencies, but impossible to imagine anybody else deviating far from the interest rate policy he pursued. The consensus in favour of the Friedmanite (not to say Keynesian) ideal policy of pursuing on-trend growth with low inflation was almost total. While people were concerned about the steady rise in debt ratios this entailed, given huge structural surpluses in savings-glut countries, would anyone, if chairman of the Fed, have deliberately slowed growth, raised unemployment above its inflation-neutral level and risked deflation just as a precaution against future debt-service problems? The answer is obviously not – and if they had, they would have been sacked, and the Fed's mandate changed by the president and/or Congress. Some of us saw what was going to happen, but within the intellectual context of the time (and probably any time) it was impossible to stop it. It was like watching a slow-motion car crash.

Likewise, we must largely absolve savings-glut countries. While collectively what they did was the primary cause of the imbalances and the debt crisis, this was not the result of any one country's unreasonable behaviour. Even the fixed exchange-rate follies that contributed so much to the imbalances were largely adopted for other, understandable reasons. It was the sum of these countries' behaviour and policies that created the problem, not any particular country. To have expected co-operation between China, Japan, the Asian Tigers and a large subsection of Europe to share out a more tolerable amount of surplus would have been absurd.

The analysis of the development of the alphabet soup of mortgage derivatives in Appendix 1 suggests where some degree of clear culpability lay:

• teaser mortgages;

- rating agencies;
- excessive profits paid out as bankers' pay rather than reserved;
- regulators' laxness in supervising capital and reserves;
- investors' sloppiness and lack of due diligence.

The underlying economics of the situation are important to this analysis. As we have seen, a steady lowering of the real rate of interest was the key indicator that excess supply of credit was the (global) driving factor, not excess demand. Yet the mortgages being created for subprime borrowers and others in the latter stages of the boom were generally at very high yields. These were (flimsily) hidden from view by the teaser mortgage structure under which payments were low in the first couple of years of the mortgage, jumping thereafter (on the assumption of refinance). Between these high yields in the mortgages being created and the low yields being accepted by investors lay a huge margin that roughly corresponded to the credit risk in the transactions. That margin should have been accumulated in the banking system's reserves as a protection against future defaults.

Instead, the MBS-CDO-CDS system transformed these mortgages into relatively low-yield instruments that were then sold by the banks to investors worldwide. These sales were made possible by dubious credit ratings from the rating agencies, whose employers were the very banks that had created the securities they were rating. The present value of that margin, which potentially lasted the full 25–30 year life of the mortgages, was therefore available to the banks, which promptly paid it out to their employees as bonuses and so on. But the banks believed their own propaganda to a great degree, and retained a surprisingly large portion of the securities. At no stage did regulators prevent or modify the banks' creation, packaging, sale or retention of these securities. Nor did they insist on the super-profits being retained as a reserve against future possible (highly likely) defaults.

The use of teaser mortgages was at best blatant self-deception on the part of mortgage brokers and the issuing banks, but clearly driven by commission structures. The interaction of the packaging banks and the rating agencies was blatantly corrupt. The pay-outs to bankers, instead of prudent reserving, was clear dereliction of the bank managements' fiduciary duty to shareholders (and, as it turned out, taxpayers that later had to bail out the banks). The negligence of the regulators was disgraceful – and is the chief area where Greenspan can be strongly criticised for his Panglossian view of senior management behaviour and attitudes.

The sloppiness of investors was inexcusable. Here again, economic forces made poor decisions hard to resist. The flood of money from savings-glut countries was driving down the real return on capital, both the real rate of interest and the yield on equities bought with fresh money. Traditional investors such as pension funds were crowded out to new asset classes – hedge funds (not an asset class, of course, but frequently described as such), private equity, even commodity derivatives – and exotic securities like mortgage-based CDOs. Both the instruments and their purveyors (investment banks as well as hedge funds) became more opaque, as the quality of the paper worsened. Rating agency imprimaturs were substituted for due diligence and credit analysis. 'Beggars can't be choosers', it was felt. But the ultimate result of this was Bernie 'Madoff with your money'. Every investor should be a chooser.

3

The crisis: policy blunders, crash and recovery

September 2007–September 2008: the year of US policy blunders

The financial crisis started in June 2007, when Merrill Lynch demanded collateral against the worsening value of assets in two Bear Stearns hedge funds that were heavily invested in mortgage-related CDOs and the like (see Appendix 1 for the alphabet soup of obscure securities). This raised the likelihood of a downward spiral of CDO prices as the hedge funds attempted to sell in a market that was illiquid to non-existent. The valuation of these CDOs was purely theoretical, based on (optimistic, going on delusory) investment bank models. In reality it was assumed they would be held to maturity, in which case, based on the rosy view being projected of likely default experience, they would yield a lifetime profit. While the entire financial community ostensibly agreed that they had value, and that the models were basically correct, the absence of liquidity – bid and offer, in particular bid – at best indicated some need for premium yield, but more probably indicated that belief in the models did not extend to staking hard cash on their conclusions.

Once it became clear that the obscure and opaque mortgage-related derivative paper was not supported by serious marketmakers, the assumptions behind a large section of the money market came unstuck. Numerous structured investment vehicles (SIVs), for example, which had been put off balance sheet by their sponsoring banks and funded as money-market mutual funds, were potentially insolvent, as they had little or no equity and depended on the valuations produced by the models to represent 100 cents in the dollar to depositors. When these valuations were no longer trustworthy, they could no longer function as off-balance-sheet funding vehicles, and had to be brought back on the balance sheets of the sponsoring banks.

Meanwhile, a lot of those banks had retained more of the mortgage and other asset-backed securities (ABSs) based derivative paper than had been supposed, especially the unrated 'toxic waste' CDO equity tranches. With a sufficient write-down – and subprime mortgage losses were potentially $¼–½ trillion at this stage – the adequacy of some banks' capital cushions could come into question, US commercial bank equity in 2007 being about $1 trillion. As all this dawned on the financial world in July and early August 2007, the willingness of banks to lend to one another plunged. This was the credit crunch. It manifested itself in a seize-up of money-market liquidity, but its cause was the questionable solvency of banks. As the crisis developed and the blight spread from subprime to prime mortgages, and the market was providing no bid for a large range of mortgage derivative instruments, the solvency issue simply grew in size and range of potentially affected institutions.

Underlying the solvency question, the crisis had arisen from too much household borrowing. Inasmuch as it stopped borrowers in their tracks, therefore, the credit crunch was part of the solution, not the problem. Any relief of the credit crunch, and the crisis generally, needed to address itself to these two points:

- attempting to revive the economy by stimulating lending, especially to households, would be wrong;
- measures to cure the banking system's liquidity seize-up had to address the questionable solvency of most institutions.

The Paulson/Bernanke team failed on both counts. Broadly, they 'left undone that which they ought to have done', and did 'that which they ought not to have done'. In Hank Paulson's case, as a former head of Goldman Sachs, he was too steeped in the merits of Wall Street's alphabet-soup bubble to see that its cover was completely blown. His understanding was consistently inadequate for the year and a half he was in charge. In Ben Bernanke's case, it was both more and less shameful. More shameful because he had understood the savings-glut theory as early as March 2005 and should have seen that it implied never-ending US debt-ratio increases that could only end in a financial crisis. Yet the Fed seems to have done no preliminary studies, nor had it any understanding of the mortgage derivative market. Less shameful is that Bernanke did see the crisis needed drastic measures.

Sadly, Bernanke chose the wrong measures – chiefly, slashing interest rates. Yet the bullish denial on both Wall Street and Main Street of the need to stop running up household debt (or any other debt) was itself only neutralised by the credit crunch. The seize-up of credit market liquidity clearly constituted a problem in that it prevented the essential roll-over of short-term debt. For that Fed liquidity was needed to give banks funding. For the Fed to cut interest rates while Wall Street was still bullish, taking stocks to their peak in October 2007 and holding them close to those peaks thereafter, was a deep misunderstanding of the issue. The Fed talked of restimulating the economy by means of rate cuts – for example, after the October 2007 rate cut: 'Today's action, combined with the policy action taken in September, should help forestall some of the adverse effects on the broader economy that might otherwise arise from the disruptions in financial markets and promote moderate growth over time.' But lower interest rates might stimulate economic growth only, or largely, through greater credit, exactly the opposite of what an economy with an excessive debt load needed. This was the classic 'cure' of reviving an alcoholic with whisky.

The sharp cuts in rates were not just inappropriate, but also seriously damaging. Partly this sprang from the fallacy of Bernanke's comparison with the 1930s crash, the subject of his academic studies. Obsessed with banking system collapse, he quickly made the financial community aware that its avoidance was the only priority of policy, never mind the dollar or inflation. Global investors took the hint and flew from the dollar into anything and everything – euros, yen, yuan futures, and so on – but notably initiating the final, vertical-ascent, phase of the oil price bubble with similar, if lesser increases in other commodity derivatives. Oil prices doubled between June 2007 and July 2008, while the Commodity Research Bureau's (US$) foodstuffs index rose by one-third. Figure 12 shows the progress of the real crude price since the current upswing started in February 1999 compared with the similar upswing in the oil crises of the 1970s. The extravagance of the 2008 spike is clear.

In effect, 2008's commodity price bubble imposed the

Figure 12   **Real oil prices in two booms**
Deflated to 'real' using US CPI

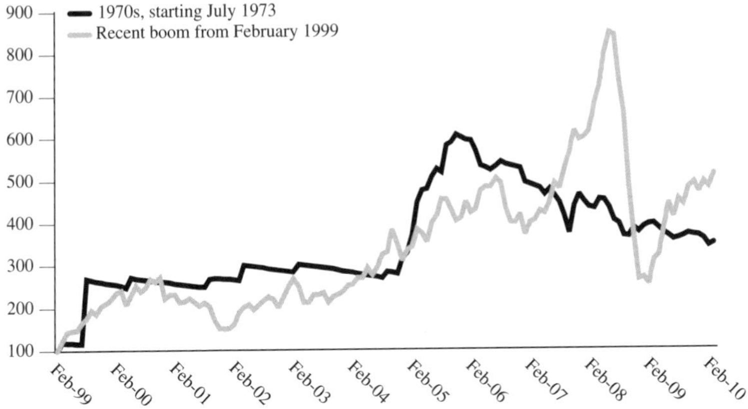

- 1970s, starting July 1973
- Recent boom from February 1999

Source: Federal Reserve Bank of St Louis

equivalent of a 2% sales tax on the world's consumers, only offset to the extent that they were commodity producers – a minor point considering that oil prices were the bulk of the price effect and oil producers are slow to spend their income gains. This unnecessary extra food-energy price effect, in addition to core inflation of CPIs between the third quarter of 2007 and the third quarter of 2008, was 2.6% for the US, 1.4% for the euro zone, 1.8% for Japan and 2.1% for Britain. For advanced economies in aggregate, real income was cut by 2%, largely as a result of Bernanke's mistake. Ironically, obsession with the Depression led him to the equivalent of what has been most criticised in policy at that time. Just as tightening budgets deflated demand in the early 1930s, Bernanke's panicky, precipitate rate cuts hammered real incomes in the year after the credit crunch struck. Maybe there was going to be a recession anyhow, but this policy made it much worse.

So much for what was done. What about what was left undone (that ought to have been done)? Before the crisis, many of us thought financial debt was simply interposed between final borrowers and lenders, of minor significance in itself. Thus the $3 trillion of mortgages held in private-sector vehicles that had issued ABSs were 20% of the 100% or so of GDP that was financial-sector debt. This seemed like a simple pass-through. It was not. The principal chain of potential grief in the banking system turned out to be default on mortgages, leading to reduced value of ABSs, knocking on to reduced values of the CDOs, which are themselves an assembly of ABSs. Thus from the disastrous 2007 batches of CDOs, triple-A securities came to be valued at around 25 cents in the dollar and triple-B as low as 3–4 cents. The equity tranches had no price.

The financial crisis was perpetuated chiefly by the pervasive financial-sector suspicion that no bank could be relied on by its depositors to lack solvency risk arising from holdings of mortgaged-backed derivatives of one sort or another. This led to banks' refusal to accept one another's credit: the credit crunch. Banks worldwide had to fund themselves with a mixture of retail deposits (effectively guaranteed by governments in most countries) and central bank liquidity help (clearly financed by governments). Paulson and Bernanke failed to grasp the weakness on the asset side of banks' balance sheets.

What ought to have been done – for the financial crisis and system, the economy being a separate matter – was to address the mutual suspicion of the banks as to one another's solvency. Shortly after the start of major liquidity provisions to the money markets, in autumn 2007, the Fed could and should have placed a requirement on the banks to:

- provide information on mortgages, the make-up of MBSs in terms of their constituent mortgages, and likewise the make-up of CDOs and other mortgage derivatives in terms of constituent MBSs;
- provide analytical and research resources to enable mortgage default scenarios to be traced through to their effects on MBSs and CDOs, and so on, and thus
- establish the information base for valuation based on reasonable scenarios, and thus two-way trading, in these obscure instruments.

In simpler parlance, the Fed should have knocked heads. Did it have the power to do so? Certainly – at least with respect to banks wanting any help with liquidity, which was virtually all of them. Is there any known instance of the Fed taking a strong line on such a matter that is clearly of public importance and within its purview, and being refused by the banks? No. How long would the research and analysis programme have taken? Probably at least six months. (Treasury Department personnel involved in implementing Paulson's eventual, year-later, autumn 2008 TARP powers were said to be upset by how difficult the valuation process was.) Was there any evidence of US Treasury or Fed contingency planning for these mortgage problems? No.

The key point here is that the financial sector's problems lay on the asset side, not on the liability side. The freeze-up of the interbank market made the liability side the place where the pain was first felt. But the source of the freeze-up was severe doubts about asset values, and therefore banks' solvency. In the absence of a proper two-way market in these assets, the bulk of the low volume of deals that did occur was instigated by firms engaged in 'fire-sale' disposals. For example, in summer 2008, Merrill Lynch cleared out its mortgaged-backed CDOs at prices around

22–23 cents in the dollar. Those who did not have to sell refused to do so at such prices, which meant that those who might have wished to buy (especially if given better information) could not do so. Meanwhile, with the requirement to mark assets to market prices, the low, fire-sale prices in the few deals actually struck, or on brokerage screens, imposed huge capital losses on banks, almost certainly exaggerated relative to the likely eventual mortgage defaults (large though those have been, or will be).

The US authorities' failure to address the key systemic problem in the year from autumn 2007 set the stage for the financial crisis. In the absence of a top-down federally enforced market-making exercise in mortgage-related assets, game-theory/Darwinian principles came into play – the law of the jungle. Weak banks kept their cards close to their chest, in the hope of being able to work out their problems without being too badly exposed, or even in the hope that 'something would turn up'. Strong banks played a waiting game, hoping (with good reason, as it turned out) to be able to pick up good strategic businesses at low prices in due course.

The authorities' lack of readiness was evident at every stage. A half-year in, with the Bear Stearns crisis in March 2008, the world was suddenly informed that the Bear's position at the centre of a web of derivatives meant it could not be allowed to go bankrupt. The Fed accepted $29 billion of downside-only risk on the Bear's junk assets to facilitate JPMorgan's acquisition of a juicy strategic brokerage business at a low price. Yet six months later (early September) the idea that such an investment bank could not be let go was reversed in the case of Lehman Brothers' bankruptcy, and then reversed again a few days later in favour of rescuing AIG. Lehman's assets in liquidation were gratefully snapped up by Barclays (US assets) and Nomura (European business). AIG was simply a ludicrously risky hedge fund holding company bobbing atop a sea of solvent and fire-walled insurance companies – thanks be for state insurance regulators, and national ones in other countries.

After the nakedness of policy was revealed in September 2008, Paulson proposed the Troubled Assets Relief Program (TARP). Under this, he hoped to sidestep the need to establish a proper trading market in mortgage-backed CDOs, etc, by conducting Dutch auctions to buy them from such banks that wished to dispose of them (notably Citibank). But this idea quickly foundered, and Paulson shifted TARP's emphasis to CDOs based on auto loans, an altogether less complex area. The problems with the original idea – aside from perfectly sound objections in principle to this particular form of nationalisation – were at least two: without the hard work of valuation of CDOs, etc, described above, the US Treasury was as much in doubt about how much it ought to pay as anybody else, and could not afford to be seen to be 'ripped off by the Street'; yet a Dutch auction procedure was likely to ensure low prices for the troubled assets, implying only the most troubled banks would use the facility, so that they would be back in the fire-sale trap with threatened solvency.

It is small wonder that after all the fuss – and claims that the absence of TARP would condemn the world to Armageddon, or at least a new Depression – Paulson simply dropped the plan, and spent the $250 billion he had been granted by the US Congress on bank shares instead: quite possibly a good investment, but hardly what had been proposed as crucial. Lastly, we had a US federal institution that emerged with credit from the crisis – the Federal Deposit Insurance Corporation (FDIC), headed by Sheila Bair

– financing a Citigroup rescue that ring-fenced and underpinned its over $300 billion of junk assets. With individual banks having done the homework needed to identify their junk, this rescue illustrates how the database to establish a trading market could have been developed.

The point was not that a two-way trading market was needed in CDOs, etc, to identify who *was* bankrupt – it was to identify who *was not* bankrupt. The insolvent institutions needed rescue, as the Citibank example demonstrated, but the system needed to get back to normal money-market business between the banks that were not insolvent. This, not some misguided revival of bank lending to the already overborrowed general public, should have been the goal of policy. But the combination of Paulson, who was imbued with belief in liquid markets as a fact of nature rather than a construct of man, and Bernanke, an academic who did not understand how the financial markets worked, was a disaster.

The financial crash

Events moved fast after the palpable muddle of Lehman/AIG, clearly demonstrating that the US authorities did not have a clue what was going on and had lost control. No detailed description of the crash and recession is needed here. But relevant aspects of them can help point up the policies and prospects now that a tentative recovery has been achieved. The stockmarkets had gone up for four months after the first major stirrings of crisis in June 2007, encouraged by Bernanke's aggressive easing: the 'Greenspan put' was still in action, it seemed. Between the October 2007 peak and the Friday before the Lehman crisis weekend (11 months) the US

S&P 500 index fell 20% and the MSCI World index (in dollars) 23%. As the informal definition of a bear market is a 20% fall, this only just qualified, though the markets had been almost as low in March 2008, when the Bear Stearns debacle gave a fore-taste of what was to come.

In just over two months from that Friday, the S&P 500 fell another 40%, a total drop of 52% from the 2007 peak; the MSCI World fell 40% too, a total drop of 54% from its peak. The November 20th 2008 trough was not the low point, however. In panics on this scale, some people inevitably get left behind. Both market indices recovered by 23–24% between then and early January, buoyed partly by hopes for the new US administration. The people left behind took their chance and sold, and in any case the fever of bank stock selling was still intensifying. By March 9th 2009, the nadir for the S&P, it had lost 27% from its early January recovery crest, and was 10% below the November low point, a total crash of 57% from the 2007 peak; for the MSCI World the March nadir was also down 27% from early January, and 11% below the November low point, a total crash of 59% from the 2007 peak. This crash had been more rapid even than the post-1929 crash, although that one ended up taking the S&P down by 84% over three years. (For perspective, reflect that a 57% loss leaves you with 43% of your money, whereas an 84% loss leaves 16%, two-fifths as much.)

The US policy shambles left the rest of the world in the lurch. Leaving aside the fact that world markets were taking a bigger beating than the S&P (as so often before in bear markets) the rest of the world was also a major investor in the epicentre of the financial earthquake – the mortgage derivative market. Not least because of the imprimatur of the questionably corrupt rating agencies, banks in much of the world were heavily exposed to these securities. And in many countries, notably Britain, Ireland and Spain, banks had their own domestic bad debt problems to worry about, on top of US mortgages. So within three weeks of the Lehman debacle, with Paulson touting his TARP to little effect, the Europeans cried 'sauve qui peut' and extended state guarantees to their own banks. Ireland moved first, in early October, quickly followed by Germany and Britain. The Netherlands and Belgium followed suit as Fortis, the recent foolish purchaser of ABN Amro at an excessive price, became insolvent, and nobody doubted that French banks were ultimately branches of the state in any case.

In effect, the US had got to the same place – comprehensive credit support for the entire banking system. AIG was guaranteed, as were the chief federally sponsored mortgage packagers, Fannie Mae and Freddie Mac, and the capabilities of the FDIC were rapidly extended. The stockmarket sell-offs of bank shares rumbled on until March, but Bernanke's Fed, unlike Paulson's Treasury, had shifted to the policy stance that would save the day from mid-September onwards. The worst of the financial crisis, as opposed to the stockmarket valuation of bank stocks, was over by Christmas.

Quantitative easing: financial market recovery

The chief sources of *potential* liquidity in the markets were twofold: short-covering and direct government action to support key markets, renamed quantitative easing (QE). While much of the selling, especially at the height of the panic from mid-September to mid-December, was by investors seeking liquidity or by debt-burdened or hedge-fund forced sellers, such conditions encouraged large numbers of cannier investors to sell the market without owning the stocks: by 'repos', stock-borrowing or futures, they went 'short'. Their profits, as prices fell, could only be crystallised by buying back. Such profits could, of course, quickly disappear if the market rallied. Short positions are notoriously difficult to manage, as any losses are not simply a bad investment but a pure, unnecessary waste of capital. Moreover, while the profit is limited to 100% of the value of the assets sold, the loss, should the price go up, is potentially unlimited. So short positions represent a major potential source of liquidity in a bear market.

QE is a new name for an old technique, debt management, vulgarly referred to as 'printing money'. If the government – or in this case more likely the Fed – buys securities in the open market from (non-bank) investors, it funds itself with short-term loans from the banks, and the investors deposit the money (received from the sale of the securities to the Fed) with the banks. So the balance sheet of the banking system is expanded on both the asset and the liability side by the transactions. As the broad money supply largely consists of bank deposits, money has, in effect, been created – hence the phrase 'printing money'.

QE is a more general form of debt management that used to be a standard technique of monetary policy. Governments usually have a large volume of debt outstanding anyhow. Some of it may be short-term, typically Treasury bills, for example with a three-month maturity. Most of it is long-term, reaching out in maturity to 30 years for the long bond in the US Treasury debt market. If the government buys back some of its long bonds (for example) and funds the purchase with bills, the bills will nearly all be held by the banks, whereas long bonds are typically not held by banks. So the investors who held them will deposit the cash they receive from their sale with the banks, matching the banks' increased assets in the form of the bills. The broad money supply will have gone up by the value of the transaction. If the government (or central bank) wants to tighten monetary policy – restricting the economy to curb inflation, for example – it can do the reverse: issue new long bonds and redeem the bills. None of this need have any implications for the short-term interest rate, which the government or central bank also controls. So it is an entirely separate tool of monetary policy, though one that has been neglected, in both university teaching and central-bank policies, in the arid and complacent world of the 1990s and 2000s (except, to some degree, in troubled Japan).

Where the government has a deficit, the means by which it funds its deficit is in any case an implicit form of QE, or QT (quantitative tightening). If all the deficit is funded with Treasury bills, the money supply will be boosted, as the government's spending in the economy (net of tax receipts) is deposited with banks and matches their purchases of the Treasury bills the government funds itself with. However, if the deficit is funded with long-maturity bonds sold to non-bank investors, the money created by the net spending will be sucked directly back into the government, and money supply will not be increased – typically leading to lesser stimulus from the deficit. In normal conditions, governments running a deficit will, or should, therefore use debt management to enhance their goals by managing the monetary consequences of their deficit.

In September 2008, the Fed reached into its toolbox and rescued debt management from the neglect of the previous 30 years or so.

Put simply, it funded itself with paper that banks normally hold and used the proceeds to buy securities. It chose its target carefully. Normally, debt management operations like this would be within the government bond market – that is, the Fed would be buying back US Treasury bonds or notes. But in this case, the Fed took the more drastic step of buying mortgage-related securities. This was an excellent decision. As we have seen, it was mortgage-related derivatives that were the black hole in the world's financial system, and it was inability to value the alphabet soup that underlay the global panic about the value of the banks. By buying mortgage-related securities, the Fed boosted – or at least supported – prices in the single most vulnerable sector of world financial markets. So it did much more than just create money.

Creating money was important too, however, as the crash involved global investor panic that drove up the demand for cash balances rather than risky securities. By creating money as well as supporting vulnerable mortgage markets, the Fed achieved two extremely valuable goals with one policy – an unusual feat. The Fed's balance sheet rose from under $1 trillion in early September 2008 to well over $2 trillion in mid-December when (rather oddly) the Fed's open-market committee announced the policy after one of its meetings. (This caused confusion, perhaps intentionally, as investors thought it was what the Fed was about to do, whereas in fact the bulk of the policy move had already occurred.) The scale of this policy shift was impressive – not far short of 10% of US GDP. So by December 2008, world markets could look forward to the back of Paulson and were benefiting from a rush of enlightenment at the Fed.

Meanwhile, the Fed funds rate, wrongly slashed in late 2007 – or rather prematurely, as it turned out – was rightly cut from

2% in early September 2008 to effectively zero in mid-December. So markets were confronted with the prospect of Fed buying, plenty of money supply to satisfy frightened investors' desire for liquid assets and zero return on such liquid assets (that is, cash) versus quite high yields in many securities markets. Moreover, the overhang of potential liquidity represented by short positions was threatened with losing its riskily earned profits in a market rally. So investors that were short bought back in and locked in their profits.

Junk bond yields, which had soared from 7½% to 17½% in the year and a half from the start of the crisis to December 12th, came down four percentage points in a month, and then junk rallied further from there. The stockmarket rallied (see page 75), though bank stock collywobbles took it down to a new low in March before the decisive spring rally. The acute part of the financial crisis was over, though the patient has been changed forever. Convalescence and recuperation will take years, and full recovery will depend on changes to economic policies that are the main subject of this book, and seem unlikely to be handled as well as one could hope.

QE prevented a simple plunge into a Depression-style financial market crash, not just by stopping the descent just in time, but by putting in place policies that ensured that, with proper analysis restored, stock prices would bounce back to the 25–30%, one-quarter to one-third, loss from 2007 peaks that was deserved, rather than the near 60% that was seen at the worst point in the crash. That rebound, from 43% of the peak (down 57%) to 70% of the peak (off 30%), was more than a 50% gain and one of the sharpest stockmarket rallies in history (matching the similar pace on the downside).

Eurasian savings gluttons' policy blunder: complacency

As analysed here, the early stages of the recession were worsened (indeed partly triggered) by the US blunder in prematurely slashing interest rates, provoking the upsurge of oil and other prices that hammered consumer incomes worldwide. But the three great Eurasian savings gluttons, China, Japan and Germany, made a blunder just as damaging in its consequences for them and the world as any made by the US. They assumed that the crisis, being a debt crisis, did not concern them. If any of them had heard of the savings-glut idea – that excessive saving was crucial to the scale of the debt crisis – they had dismissed it. It did not occur to them that their growth, based on net export surplus, and therefore on net imports elsewhere, required that someone somewhere else would have to be borrowing the money to buy their goods; and that their build-up of overseas assets involved some other person in some other country accruing liabilities. If that someone got into trouble through having borrowed too much, those net imports would be cut, and with them the net exports of savings gluttons. In other words, the credit crunch marked the beginning of the end of either their growth or their ability to sustain a savings glut. The 'habits of a lifetime' would have to change for them, just as much as for the US, the UK, and so on.

The plight of the savings gluttons is thus a classic case of 'beware of what you wish for'. For the first 12–15 months after the subprime crisis hit in summer 2007, politicians and other commentators in continental Europe and China – less so in Japan, perhaps chastened by memories of their own dark decade of the 1990s – were quick to criticise Anglo-Saxon borrowing and spending habits. They were right, of course, particularly in relation to bankers' excesses. But, as we have seen, the blame lay (and lies) as much with the habitual oversavers as with the chronic borrowers. Without the US debt bubble being prolonged well beyond the end of 2005, for example, when US house prices peaked, Germany's dismal long-run growth record would be even worse, as would Japan's. When the savings gluttons held forth on how the borrowers should stop their bad habits, they clearly were unaware that they were condemning themselves to a violent recession.

The credit crunch meant the end of the deficit counterpart to savings gluts. Without the deficit-countries' private-sector borrowing to use the savings, the Eurasian glut turned into a global savings glut – or rather, demand deficiency. As it turned out, the countries with a structural demand deficiency – a savings glut – suffered most in the recession. Like most recessions, it was worsened on the way down by a heavy bout of inventory liquidation, so that production fell from somewhat above final demand – that is, inventory building – to well below it. But the savings-glut countries all depended on goods exports as the leading element in their economies. Inventory fluctuations in all countries tend to be strongly reflected in imports – so world trade slumped, starting to decline in earnest in November 2008. The recession, moderate in advanced countries in the middle quarters of 2008, was vicious in the descent to its trough in the first quarter of 2009, worse than the recession of 1974–75 or the double recessions of 1980 and 1982.

Recovery policies: government deficits

While recession was more severe than necessary because of late 2007 US policy blunders and savings gluttons' complacency, there was little doubt during 2008 that the US private sector would have to adjust towards higher net savings under any scenario. Whether with growth or recession, this meant lower net imports. Much the same was inevitable in Britain, Spain, Australia and other deficit nations. So the fall-out from the crisis is that healthy recovery depended on the policies of the surplus countries, in particular China, Japan and Germany, numbers 2–4 in size in the world. A healthy recovery could ensue if they reduce their net saving, which meant either structural policies to lower the private sector's excessive saving, or willing adoption of structural government deficits.

Failing such optimal surplus-country behaviour, the global recovery has depended on huge increases in government deficits, concentrated in the same deficit countries that have just overutilised their private-sector debt capacity. Such deficits are to stimulate demand and offset the need for private debt reduction. Between 2007 and 2009, the budget deficit of developed, OECD countries rose by 7% of GDP from 1.3% to 8.2%. Three-fifths of this increase (4.2 percentage points) was structural, or policy-driven, the remainder being the recession's effect on tax revenue and relief spending. These deficits account for the bulk of the recovery.

Though the worst of the recession was in the savings-glut countries, Japan and Germany did less than other OECD countries to counter its effects. The increase in Japan's structural deficit was nil in 2008 and 2.8% of GDP in 2009. Germany raised

Table 1 **World trade (import) effects of trend growth, 2008**

	GDP ($bn)	Growth trend % per year	Growth trend $bn	Approximate import ratio (%)	Implied import gain (locomotive power) $bn[a]
World	60,690	3.4	2,076	–	–
US	14,265	2.8	399	16	64
North-central Europe (NCE)[b]	7,563	1.5	113	30	34
Other Western Europe	11,780	2.5	294	25	74
Japan	4,924	1.5	74	10	7
China	4,402	9.8	431	27	116
Asian Tigers[c]	2,913	5.0	146	30	44
India	1,210	7.5	91	–	–
Other advanced	1,831	3.0	55	–	–
Other developing	11,803	4.0	472	–	–

a Using the average (approximate estimated) import ratio rather than attempting an incremental ratio.

b Germany, Benelux, Nordic countries, Switzerland, Austria; import ratio roughly eliminates intra-trade.

c Hong Kong, Indonesia, Malaysia, Philippines, Singapore, Taiwan, Thailand.

its structural deficit by a total of 1.3% of GDP over the two years to 2009 (see Table 1). These countries enjoyed a modest bounce in GDP during the second half of 2009 owing to recovery elsewhere, and in particular an easing of the inventory cycle from strong liquidation in mid-2009. This latter is, however, a temporary boost that runs out as inventory behaviour returns to normal. During 2010 and subsequently, recovery in these two countries – and the NCE countries round Germany – will largely depend on their willingness to reverse the behaviour patterns and policies of 2003–07 (see Chapters 7 and 8).

The bulk of the recovery in the second half of 2009 stemmed from strong fiscal stimulus programmes in the US, Britain, Spain, to some degree France and, more than anywhere else, China. Fortunately, in its impact on the rest of the world's economy, China is about four times more important than Germany and its surrounding NCE savers, and 15–20 times more important than Japan (see Table 1). It is even about twice as important as the US, though America's impact is greater for advanced economies. China's late 2008 stimulus of 4 trillion yuan (some 13% of 2008 GDP) was in itself probably the largest such programme in history, even including wars. But the outcome was even larger. Bank lending in just the first half of 2009 grew by 7 trillion yuan, whereas the normal rate of growth, around a 15% annual rate, would have indicated only an extra 2 trillion yuan. This 7 trillion yuan was nearly a quarter of 2008's GDP, and therefore nearly a half the half-yearly GDP in which it occurred.

In the US, the large fiscal package of the incoming Obama administration in February 2009 helped drive the structural budget deficit up by 6.1% of GDP between 2007 and 2009. Britain's structural balance shifted by 6.4% over the same two years and Spain's by 8.4%. These deficit countries were facing the direct effects of the credit crunch in stopping private borrowing, and, to avoid massive debt deflation, the extra deficits had both to provide demand stimulus and to absorb some debt from the more stricken parts of the private sector.

The effects of the fiscal stimulus in 2009, and the 2010 follow-up in some countries, reversal in others, are best looked at in the following chapters covering behaviour, policies and prospects in the various regions of the world. The summary point concerning the crisis was that just enough was done to stem the collapse of final demand and reverse the inventory cycle towards a temporary rebound. Just as the US did less badly in recession than the advanced-country savings gluttons, so it also rebounded somewhat better. China's economy has shifted with astonishing speed from slack to overheating, thanks to its violent stimulus. But the favourable impact this might otherwise have on the rest of the world is offset by its rapid gains of export market share, helped by the competitiveness arising from the cheap yuan. In early 2010, the world economy was poised between continued recovery and a renewed slowdown – but deeply vulnerable, as we shall see.

4

The fiscal crisis

The 'savings glut' concept involves the surplus of saving over investment being structural, not cyclical, reflecting deep-seated policy and behaviour. This appetite for surplus has continued to prove largely impervious to the price of money, that is, the real rate of interest or the return on capital. Although real and nominal interest rates have dived in the current recession, this is not the reason that the current surplus of savings-glut countries fell. Their recessions were export-led, as deficit countries slashed borrow-and-spend, so trade surpluses naturally fell.

For China and the Asian Tigers, a big part of this deep-seated policy or behaviour consists of the mercantilist urge toward export-led growth (see Chapter 2). For them, therefore, the current-account surplus is a fair measure of the savings glut. Within their domestic economies, relatively backward financial systems and other factors may reinforce the tendency to high savings. But the distinction between this and the policy drive towards export surplus is hard to draw, not least because (in China especially) the line between the public and the private sector is not clear.

The advanced countries with a savings glut are different. The glut is very much a private-sector behavioural phenomenon. It reflects two major trends: falling growth and often the absolute level of population, especially that of working age; and restructuring by business to improve capital productivity and/or pay down debt. The lower population growth reduces the need for investment, especially in construction. And the predominance of baby-boomers now relatively late in their careers – a high-savings period in the life cycle – means household savings tend to be high. Restructuring adds to the surplus of business cash flow over investment. So for these countries, the financial surplus of the private sector is a better measure of the savings glut than the current account of the balance of payments.

US, UK and others join the savings glut

Viewed as a private-sector surplus (for advanced countries), a savings glut has now developed in the US, Britain, Canada and most of the euro zone that is not in the NCE (the latter being part of the Eurasian savings glut to start with). These countries have switched from large private deficits in 2005–07, offsetting the Eurasian glut, to large surpluses now. Some of this switch is purely cyclical, reflecting the recession. Clearly, the private surplus in 2009 was boosted by both recessionary levels of tax payment (low) and inventory liquidation (high) – plus other lesser influences in the same direction. But equally clearly, deficit countries are going to persist with structural private-sector financial surpluses in the medium term. This is what adjustment means, given that the crisis originated with excessive private-sector, especially household, borrowing, and balance sheets now have to be rectified by several years' financial surplus.

While this observation hardly seems controversial, the

Figure 13 **Advanced countries' private-sector financial surpluses, plus China/Asian Tigers' current account**

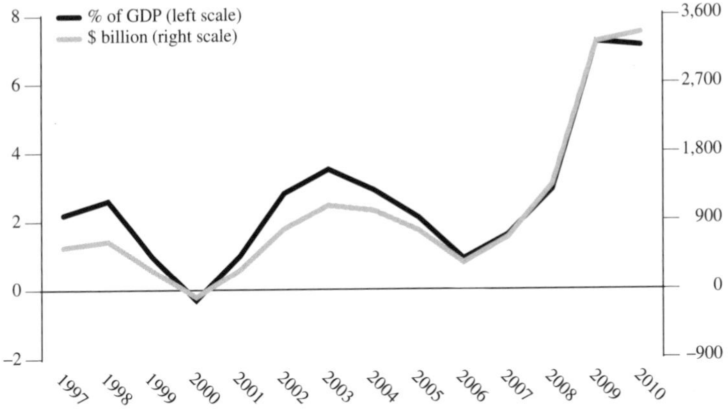

Source: OECD

dimensions and implications of the problem it creates are huge. Partly, the size of the swing is not fully appreciated – people focus on the counterpart budget deficits, not the private balance itself, let alone the extent to which it may prove structural. Partly, the fact that it has occurred in large economies, notably the US, adds heft to the cash value of the transformation and makes the global implications alarming.

The US private-sector deficit reached 3.8% of GDP in 2006; by 2009 it had reversed into an 8.2% surplus, a 12% of GDP swing. This is forecast (by the OECD) to slim down a little to a 7.3% surplus in 2010, as inventories cease to be heavily liquidated, but this still leaves an 11% swing. Perhaps recovery will cut this total swing, but even 8–9% of the US economy equals the entire Eurasian savings glut at its peak in 2007. Moreover, the US private financial balance could easily increase, rather than shrink, even on a structural basis. The household savings ratio has so far moved much less than halfway from its negligible pre-crisis level to where it probably needs to go – a substantial further measure of structural adjustment may be yet to come.

The UK private-sector balance has swung from a small deficit of 0.6% of GDP in 2006 to a surplus of 10% in 2009, with 10.9% forecast by the OECD for 2010. In Canada, the swing has been minor, but in Australia, the private financial deficit reached 8.1% of GDP in 2007 and then fell to 0.2% in 2009, with a 1% deficit forecast for 2010. In the euro zone excluding the NCE countries – that is, France, Ireland and 'Club Med' (Italy, Spain, Greece and Portugal) – the private financial deficit peaked at 2.9% of GDP in 2007, and swung into a 4.3% surplus in 2009, with 4.6% forecast for 2010 as deflationary policies kick in (though these are now much intensified after the Greek debt debacle). This 7½% swing is smaller in ratio and applies to a smaller economy than the US, but combined with the large British swing it makes a huge impact on the European economy.

The combined effect of all this is formidable, as the recession has also induced a higher private surplus in the savings-glut countries, some of which may last for some time. Advanced world economies, the US, Canada, Australia, western Europe and Japan, were close to private-sector balance in 2006 with a minimal deficit of 0.6% of GDP, as deficit countries offset the savings glut. In 2009 the surplus was 7.3%, and for 2010 the forecast is 7.6%. In cash terms the swing is from roughly nil to a massive $3 trillion.

The increase of this private surplus expected in 2010 indicates how little recovery is helping to cut it, especially outside the US. Medium-term structural adjustment is needed in Britain and in Club Med and Ireland, and the US household savings rate still has to rise significantly. This $3 trillion surplus is largely structural. The government deficits that are its prime offset also have to absorb some $400 billion of China-Asian Tiger current-account surpluses. The implicit total imbalance of $3¼–3½ trillion is 2½–3 times the peak Eurasian current-account surplus of $1¼ trillion in 2007.

Large government deficits indefinitely

The OECD puts the GDP of the advanced countries we are considering at $39 trillion in 2010. The government deficit needed to offset 2010 private surpluses, plus the current-account surpluses of China and the Tigers and net effects from the rest of the world, is $3.3 trillion, 8½% of that GDP. Since these flows are largely structural, this scale of deficit will occur for several years. It can, at the global level, be held at this level by two conceptually different approaches:

- acceptance of structural deficits at this level;
- attempts to remove deficits – probably piecemeal by country – leading to negligible growth, if not outright renewed recession, and thus a large increase in the cyclical element in the deficit as unemployment mounts.

The second of these appears far the more likely of the two, not least because the euro zone has already moved down that road. The case of Japan is special and separate (see Chapter 8). But EMU countries are devoted to cutting budget deficits under the rubric of the ill-conceived Stability and Growth Pact, with Germany in the lead, having recently passed a constitutional amendment prohibiting structural budget deficits. Club Med and Ireland are slashing budget deficits savagely. Britain is exposed to bond market pressure to follow suit, if in more moderate style. US politics are being transformed by a populist movement that blames the government for all the country's ills (though the government has within the past two years rescued both the banking system and the economy from ruin). US budget deficits are likely to come under pressure soon, and are already being cut at state and local level in response to balanced-budget laws.

When it comes to the distribution of deficits, the private-sector debt problems in the Anglo-Saxon economies mean that government deficits are much higher there. Whereas the private surplus of Japan and NCE is 10.7% of GDP, compared with 6.8% for North America, Australia and non-NCE Europe, the respective 2010 government deficits are forecast as 5.8% and 10.4% of GDP. So the Eurasian savings-glut part of the advanced economies retains a surplus (on current account) of nearly 5% of GDP, while the deficit countries have a deficit a little under 3½% of GDP. This imbalance is unlikely to prove stable. Under the first policy alternative described above – in which savings-glut countries show awareness of the damage they are causing – NCE countries in particular would be boosting government spending or cutting taxes. But we can be reasonably sure that this will happen only on a minor scale.

So reduced imbalance in the advanced world could come in two or three stages:

- Budgetary deflation in deficit countries, especially Club Med and

Figure 14 **Advanced countries' government deficits**

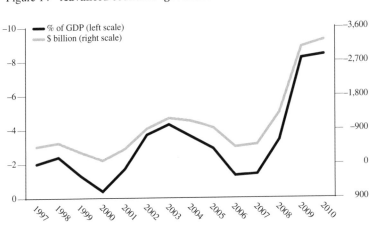

Source: OECD

Ireland, and net import reductions in the US and UK, helped by currency depreciation that permits some growth.

- Stagnation through frustration of exports, leading to rising cyclical deficits in NCE and Japan.

- The introduction of protectionist import restrictions, provoked by impatience with Chinese world trade share gains and the artificially cheap yuan exchange rate, by either the EU (driven by France and Club Med) or the US, the argument being – 'Why are we saddling our children with government debt just to support jobs in Shenzen, Shizuoka or Stuttgart?'

Assuming the protectionism threat is avoided or at least minimised, the first two stages imply a less dire outcome for North America and Australia than Japan and the EU, with Britain somewhere in between. A possible mitigating factor for the US (and perhaps other Anglo-Saxons Britain, Australia and Canada) might be equity flows. Better growth prospects than in the Eurasian savings-glut economies and the EU – crushed by balanced-budget fervour – should lead to net disinvestment from the latter and some recapitalisation of overindebted business in the Anglo-Saxons. One result should be a cut in the business subsection of the private-sector financial surplus: equity capital inflows should create a positive wealth effect, and a mix of greater capital spending and distribution of cash flow. The needed offset to this, a lesser government deficit, would arise naturally from the implicitly improved income and growth performance.

Government deficits to be readily financed

Although there has been much fuss and bother about government deficits in Club Med and Ireland, the basic truth is that most government deficits will be readily financed, even though they are likely to remain alarmingly large for a long time. The simple reason is that with private surpluses at current levels, and China and the Tigers running surpluses on top, the money has nowhere else to go – except into stocks and real estate that on a global scale are hardly going to be attractive with economies hampered if not hammered by deflationary policies. Equally clearly, the unprecedented scale of the imbalances now in play means that bond markets will remain highly volatile, as attention veers from one alarm signal to the next.

One source of volatility is that in the US and the UK the private surpluses are almost entirely concentrated in the business sector, not households. But businesses do not exist to buy government bonds. Some may pay down debt, and the investors paid off may then switch to government bonds. But some will transfer money internationally, or buy back their own stock. In the last case, the investor receiving the cash was not a natural bond buyer, but a stockholder. So the process of getting the cash from business surpluses into funding of government deficits has involved a prolongation of the stockmarket recovery (as firms buy back their own stock, or make bids for other stock) and a significant increase in the yield of government bonds, to lure investors for whom this is not the preferred type of security.

The commitment of Germany, France and the Benelux countries (the euro-zone core) to EMU means they will support Club Med and Ireland with loans or guarantees only after sharp cuts in their deficits. Within EMU, belt-tightening only means adjustment solely by huge cuts in wages. This will be violently deflationary. Belt-tightening with devaluation would quickly adjust relative wages downwards and permit the resumption of growth much sooner. To keep Club Med in the euro, the core countries have to stump up cash or guarantees. Deflation will be savage. Time will tell if countries will tolerate this. The Club-Med/Irish bond market crisis is not about whether their government deficits can or will be financed – it is about whether they stay in the euro. Their departure would impose major losses on investors in their bonds (mostly German and French banks, it is reported). It is fear of such losses that underlies the current crisis, as well as doctrinal political commitment to the euro.

As for the US, the probable shift of the CPI from very low inflation now to deflation over the next year or two (see Chapter 6) will give the lie to the hysterical talk of impending inflation there. The likelihood of a serious upswing of inflation with unemployment close to 10% and likely to stay high is precisely zero. Meanwhile, the US has three major advantages in the funding of its deficit:

- The large and liquid Treasury bond market is *ipso facto* far the most attractive resort for the huge western private-sector and China/Tiger surpluses seeking a home.
- The dollar is far and away the pre-eminent reserve currency, and will therefore perform its usual role of safe haven in the difficult financial times the world will be going through.
- China, as long as the yuan is pegged to the dollar, is a forced, cram-down investor in dollars. Major attempted diversification would simply create upward pressure on the yuan rate that would force it to buy back the dollars.

China's public complaints about the dollar have been a convenient bluff. The weakness of the dollar in 2009 served China well, carrying down the yuan and creating rapid gains in export market share to the benefit of the country's recovery vis-à-vis that of others. Of course, this motivates the Chinese authorities to continue moaning about the dollar in public – though it is not clear whether they are cunning, or just lucky. Anyhow, China is lucky to have the dollar as the chief outlet for its unjustifiable surpluses. Germany gets to pour its net export gains down the drain in Greece, Portugal, and so on. Japanese private surpluses finance dubious investments in Japanese government bonds. The current situation carries little identifiable threat over the next few years either to the US government's ability to finance its deficits or to the dollar as reserve currency.

A weaker link in the government credit chain is Britain. What it needs at the moment is a tighter fiscal policy and a lower real exchange rate. (This has not always been true – heavy overvaluation served Britain well in 1997–2007.) The problem is that decisive moves to tighten the budget balance would probably cheer bond vigilantes and raise the exchange rate – the reverse of what is needed. Unlike the US with China, or Greece with the eurozone core, Britain lacks a natural financier to fund its deficit. It is also, of course, an order of magnitude smaller than the US (though also an order of magnitude larger than Greece) and not in possession of a reserve currency. So a spillover of the Club Med government debt crisis to the UK is possible. This could be a good thing: it would ensure a lower exchange rate and enforced cuts in the budget deficit – exactly the combination needed. The new coalition government, however, seems set on a policy of cutting the deficit – so Britain could in fact reinforce the lurch of Europe towards depression.

Japan already has deflation; NCE will get it soon; the US and Club Med could follow next year, and perhaps eventually Britain, despite the knock-on effect of large recent devaluation. So the inflation element in government bond yields (the difference between conventional and inflation-linked bond yields) could fall to extremely low levels. Partly offsetting this in the near term could be higher real interest rates, as the sheer volume of government issuance cuts their bonds' credit rating vis-à-vis high-grade corporates (or governments with little or no issuance like Sweden or Switzerland).

Could the need for the large private financial surpluses that are forcing governments into deficit be reduced by structural measures? Fiscal or other incentives would have to attempt to:

- cut personal savings propensities;
- increase housing investment;
- cut business profitability;
- increase business investment ratios to GDP.

Japan's personal savings are already small, owing to the large 1930s generation having great longevity and being now retired (Chapter 8). A similar tendency could be expected in Europe, once the baby-boomers retire. But the baby boom really got going after the Erhard reforms of 1948 had restarted the German economy, that is, from 1950 onwards. People born in 1950 reach 65 in 2015, and talk of mass early retirement in Germany is much exaggerated. To be sure, the working-age population is declining, by 3.4% over the ten years to 2009, for example. But over the same period, the labour force participation rate has increased rapidly, from 74.8% to 80.5%. (The choice of period does not affect the argument significantly.) As a result, the labour force was up by 4%, increased participation having more than twice the impact of age-group shrinkage. So a significant downward shift in savings rates from baby-boomers shifting out of late-career high saving into full spending of their retirement income (as has already happened to a great degree in Japan) is unlikely before 2015 in Germany or elsewhere in Europe.

Meanwhile, in the US, and to a degree in Britain, the opposite tendency is likely. Inadequate private-pension provision, as well as pushing up the savings rate in the next few years, could also postpone the age of effective retirement beyond 65 to whatever age is needed to make up for past shortfalls in pension provision. So the basic trend in personal savings could be positive for many years. As for housing, especially in the US, it is clear that a major recovery in spending is unlikely for years, owing to the excesses of the recent boom. Nor do population trends suggest much recovery elsewhere in advanced countries, so structural reduction of the household element of the private-sector financial surplus is improbable for five years at least.

Can we – should we – expect (or hope for) lower business profitability to cut into the current, seemingly natural, global private-sector savings glut? The answer is probably yes, but only gradually. The only country of the largest five advanced countries whose profit ratio appeared high in 2007–08 – beyond the peak-of-boom, cyclical effect – is Germany. But between then and 2010, profit ratios had already been cut sharply in the recession, especially in Germany, where policies have focused the loss of income particularly heavily on business. So the chief reason for expecting lower profit ratios over time is the structural downward pressure from excess saving and slow growth. Allied to this, the erosion of market shares by Chinese exports and excessive Chinese capacity installation are part of the logical chain by which excess savings supply provokes a lower return on capital. So the chief hope for reducing the world's private financial balances lies in erosion of business profitability – not a reassuring route.

On the business investment front, the secular force we can count on is Chinese and other emerging markets being the main locus of future investment growth and, since they finance such investment out of their own savings, not acting as a useful outlet for the excess private savings of advanced countries. In a normal cycle, the years after 2010 should produce some upswing of business investment in advanced economies. But it is hard to see where the initial demand comes from to provoke such a recovery, as government deficit stimulus is exhausted and, if anything, is likely to be a negative influence from now on. Monetary growth, for sure, is a major block to recovery, as advanced economies' broad money has been growing at less than 1%. Bank take-up of government debt merely offsets shrinkage of loans to the debt-reducing private sector. So this fourth possible source of spending, and at least cyclical reduction of private surplus, cannot be depended on for much in the next 2–3 years.

The forward projection of the multiple factors involved in taking a view on how this global private-sector savings glut, and resulting government deficits, might develop is clearly hazardous. But without major acceptance of structural government deficit expansion in Japan and NCE – and/or a seismic shift in China towards yuan appreciation and reorientation to a market-based domestic economy – the prospects for global growth over the next few years are extremely poor. Government deficits unprecedented in peacetime are with us to stay, and likewise the build-up of government debt. My original, September 2004 Monthly Review expressing the Eurasian savings-glut idea was carefully entitled *US balance sheets to be serially trashed by Eurasian savings excesses*. The meaning of that title was that business balance sheets were trashed in the 1998–2000 bubble, household balance sheets were being trashed in 2003–07, and that government balance sheets would then be trashed. The latter process is now well under way.

5

China's surge and relapse

The three great savings-glut countries, China, Japan and Germany, numbers 2–4 in size in the world, have responded in very different ways to the financial crisis. Hapless Japan, the original savings glutton from the 1990s, verges on helpless, with entrenched and intensifying deflation, huge existing government indebtedness and large structural deficits (see Chapter 8). Germany has been defensive, with modest spending programmes and tax cuts; the hope (probably vain) is that the country can return to export-led growth-as-usual (see Chapter 7). Only China has stepped up to the challenge of a committed stimulus to domestic demand.

Fortunately, in its impact on the rest of the world's economy, China is about four times more important than Germany and its surrounding savers of north-central Europe, and 15–20 times more important than Japan (see the last column in Table 1 on page 84). China's end-2008 stimulus of 4 trillion yuan (some 13% of 2008 GDP) caused bank lending in just the first half of 2009 to grow by nearly 7 trillion yuan. Its normal rate of growth, around a 15% annual rate, would have indicated only an extra 2 trillion yuan.

Chinese exports fell by 25–30% in volume (more in value

– export prices were declining) between October 2008 and spring 2009. To judge by the official real growth statistics this had remarkably little impact. But few close observers believe the official real growth numbers. Reworking the data using the more plausible nominal GDP numbers and various price indices, Lombard Street Research calculations suggest that China's real GDP fell an extremely sharp 7% or so in just two quarters: 2008 Q1 and 2009 Q4. This is a much more plausible picture, given the extremely aggressive policy response – with a flavour almost of panic.

China's quarterly real GDP growth estimates are not anchored by reference to levels of price-adjusted quarterly GDP. As well as preventing any analysis of quarterly movements (seasonally adjusted or not), this frustrates independent analysis. However, China publishes a much less publicised run of nominal quarterly data that better match other relevant numbers than do the real quarterly growth rates. Price changes are also given, generally in year-on-year form but sometimes as indices: for the CPI and non-food CPI, for various forms of fixed investment (including construction), and for exports and imports. These can be turned into estimated price indices for those parts of GDP. Using the weights of consumption, fixed investment, exports and imports in domestic demand and GDP, I have calculated composite indices for the price level of domestic demand and GDP back to the first quarter of 2004. Applying these price indices to the seasonally adjusted nominal series gives a quarterly real series. Because the procedure is estimated without the inside information available to official statisticians, the conclusions below are probably correct in order of magnitude, though not to the decimal point (which is avoided where possible).

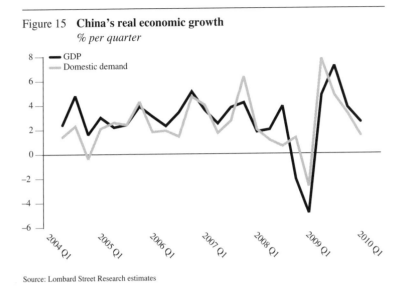

Figure 15   **China's real economic growth**
% per quarter

Source: Lombard Street Research estimates

Figure 15 shows that real domestic demand bounced back a torrid 8% in just Q2 alone, and 5% in Q3 – 13% in just two quarters (a 28% annual rate as Americans present such statistics). As a result, GDP grew 5% in Q2 and 7% in Q3 – more than 12% in the two quarters together (a 26% annual rate). This was an astonishing result. One point is that 12% over two quarters is 7% ahead of trend growth (10% annually, that is, 5% over two quarters). So China's nearly 3% of slack in the economy at the start of 2009, at the worst of the recession, was replaced by 4% of overheating by Q3. The economy continued with an above-trend 4% real quarterly GDP increase in Q4, when GDP was 5–6% above its 25-year real trend. In 2010 Q1, growth settled down to an on-trend 2½% (a 10% annual rate) but that meant that the accumulated 5–6% shift above trend, that is overheating, remained in place.

As well as being overwhelming in size – and threatening a

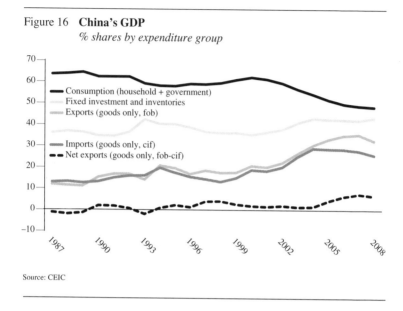

Figure 16 **China's GDP**
% shares by expenditure group

Source: CEIC

major lurch back into inflation – China's stimulus seemed misdirected. The emphasis was and is almost entirely on excessive and wasteful domestic investment. What China needs is much higher consumption, as household and government consumption combined amount to only 49% of GDP. The national savings rate, however, is a mountainous 51% – comprising 8% of net export surplus and 43% of domestic investment (plus net service exports, which the data do not separate out). Even in a country with a 10% real growth trend, a 43% investment ratio is about one-fifth wasted. China has its own answer to Japan's famous examples of government waste (those 'bridges to nowhere' and 'vegetable airports') – 'highways to the Gobi desert'.

But alarm in the winter of 2008–09 about the vulnerability of the economy to a crash in exports meant that the 8% net export surplus was the immediate focus of policy. And the quickest way for the government to narrow this net-export gap between 51% consumption and 43% investment was to raise the 43% investment rate, the urge to consume being even more depressed than usual by the recession. So – more highways to the Gobi desert.

The waste is clearest when it comes to infrastructure. China already has good infrastructure for its level of income. Electricity generation is a good example. Its economy is about 3½ times that of Britain at purchasing-power parity, and British generating capacity is around 84 gigawatts with about industrial-country average power usage vis-à-vis GDP. Yet China installed an average of 92 GW a year in 2005–08, almost doubling total capacity to 793 GW, nearly ten times that of Britain. So why install more? Electricity is subsidised, encouraging overinvestment and waste, often in seriously polluting industries such as aluminium smelting.

In roads, China's expressway system at 60,000 kilometres is three-quarters the length of the US interstate highways, with only one-quarter of the cars. Yet Chinese mileage has doubled in the past five years, and is expected to be twice that of the US in ten years' time. While the number of cars on the road may well grow fast, this cannot be a productive use of capital. In effect, excessive saving is forcing wasteful investment, driving down the return on capital. Similar wastage in Japan from the mid-1990s onwards was a significant contributor to the drastic slowing of its trend growth to 1%, from 4½% in the 1980s.

Waste is one thing; bubbles are quite another. In mid-2009 the concern was that wasteful investment and excessive industrial capacity installation would slow China's growth trend and deflate the world economy via the downward pressure on prices of severely underutilised capacity, not just in China but in most of the industrial world. These are still concerns, but two other shifts – as usual with China, extremely large and rapid – have overtaken them as priorities. First, a huge surge in housing and other building has raised the question: is China finally going to generate its own housing bubble, with eventual, inevitable collapse? Second, with the yuan effectively heavily devalued in 2009 by its link to the dollar, exports have rebounded so strongly from their collapse between autumn 2008 and spring 2009 that their combination with booming domestic demand threatens immediate and inflationary overheating.

Taking the second point first, inflation in China would hardly surprise a monetarist. While the monthly growth of bank loans and broad money (M2) has slowed since June, their 12-month growth rate accelerated to 30%, and remained well above 20% in the early months of 2010. The monthly pace of change has slowed significantly, but it remains around 20% annually, still well above the longer-run average of 15–17%. Meanwhile, the slippage of the dollar, to which the yuan has been pegged since spring 2008 at 6.83, had knocked more than 10% off China's trade-weighted exchange rate by late 2009, although the recent recovery of the dollar has partly reversed that. Such a devaluation with 20–30% monetary growth would normally be expected to generate inflation. Even with a growth trend of 10%, the most intense monetisation of a backward, barter economy cannot justify such monetary stimulus.

By early 2010, China's export volume had rebounded to about equal its summer 2008 peak. By contrast, Japan's and Germany's were still about 15% lower than pre-crash peaks. China is enjoying a large gain in world trade share, partly aided by devaluation. The pace of gains has slowed as the global inventory snap-back

Figure 17   **China's building sales/starts**
Sq. m., 12-month % change

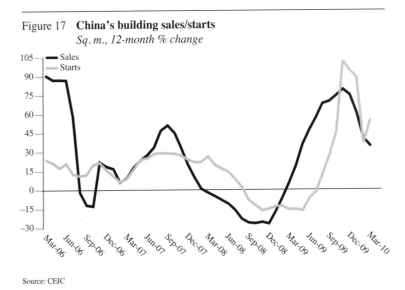

Source: CEIC

has largely finished, but real export growth is still 4% on a quarterly basis. This is about 1½% of GDP in export growth per quarter, given exports still above one-third of GDP. Even allowing for around a 40% import content in exports, this growth of net exports alone uses up two fifths of the 2½% non-inflationary quarterly GDP growth trend. So little space is left for increased domestic demand.

Returning to the housing bubble issue, domestic demand is still growing, so overheating should be followed by rapidly accelerating inflation. The wasteful infrastructure projects were being launched during 2009; they cannot readily be just switched off. Apart from these, the prime form of response to the stimulus package has been in real estate and housing. Where else could the 7 trillion yuan of extra credit in early 2009 expend itself? (The gain in domestic demand over the second and third quarters of 2009 amounted to only one-tenth of that amount.) From the peak in summer/autumn 2007, building sales were down about a quarter by a year later, but by the end of 2009 they were up 80%. On an index basis, after falling from 100 to 75, they had risen to around 130–35 – up by one-third in two years, in other words, from what were already, two years ago, peak levels. The year-on-year growth rate slowed sharply to 40% in early 2010, but that is to a great degree an effect of the unusual timing of the Chinese New Year, and the fact that early 2009 was a less depressed base for comparison than late 2008. The point is that growth may now be slower, but it is starting from an already elevated level after the surge during 2009.

Where sales go, there follow prices, and then building starts. So prices started to move up significantly in the spring. Building starts show a lag of about six months from sales, but in late 2009 they rocketed to levels nearly double those at the end of 2008. Here again the rate of growth fell sharply to 40–50% in early 2010, but such growth is now proceeding from a higher level. As starts had been down only 15% the year before, this meant the autumn/winter level of starts has been up some 40% on two years earlier. Rapidly growing building activity should last well into 2010 at least.

Major cyclical swings in real estate and construction do not necessarily imply bubbles. It is a strongly cyclical industry in most countries and periods. In principle, if the housing sales were largely for owner-occupation, this housing boom would be the single best aspect of the recent Chinese recovery, as housing activity is more closely related to consumption than other forms of investment, and leads to extra consumption anyhow as people furnish their homes. Also an owner-occupied housing boom would imply rapid growth of the mortgage market, which is the single strongest instrument for transferring savings from older, high-saving households to younger ones, thus using up savings within the personal sector and lowering the aggregate of personal saving.

There are two problems with the rosy implications of this scenario. First, there is strong anecdotal evidence that much of the housing purchases are investments, some of them debt-financed, and that affordability is poor for owner-occupier buyers (bearing in mind that Chinese incomes are a fraction of those in the West). Second, such investment is vulnerable to the monetary tightening that inevitably results from overheating and the revival of significant inflation.

A portion of purchases seem to have been made by investors using the explosion of credit to attempt leveraged gains on real estate. This is consistent with the huge excess of credit growth relative to domestic demand growth, an excess that had to be channelled at least partly into asset markets. It is also attractive for investors whose only alternatives are a violently fluctuating stockmarket (which also soared in the January-August period and then relapsed) and state-owned bank deposits yielding 1–2% at the short end, rising to 3.6% for five years.

Many of these newly purchased investment properties are said to be empty. This is a classic bubble symptom: investors are relying for their profit on capital gains from the greater fool they eventually expect to sell to. In China, with little memory of real estate busts and strong official encouragement of lax lending practices, the results could be particularly virulent. Maintenance charges are low, and interest rates have been low since the crash, so the monthly cost of holding an empty property is low right now. But inflation is accelerating fast, so interest rates will soon have to be raised, probably a long way. At that stage, holding an empty property could become a major financial burden, or at best a large opportunity cost for debt-free investors.

The rapid shift towards overheating leaves the government with three options: accept accelerating inflation, cut domestic demand, or cut export demand. But the only major influence it has over the latter is via the exchange rate. It would be easy to please the foreigners exerting huge pressure for yuan appreciation. But the government sees export industry success as the foundation of China's economic success, and the export industries, through their agency, the Commerce Department, are in any case the strongest lobby in Beijing. The shock of export collapse in late 2008 and early 2009 is fresh in the mind, so no threat to export recovery is taken lightly. Moreover, westerners have presented the exchange rate issue in terms of what China should do for the West. In the communist mentality, economics is a zero-sum game, so there could be a tendency for officials to see it as 'they want it, so it must be bad for us'. However, the argument for yuan appreciation is that it helps China in several ways:

- There would be a slower build-up of useless dollar reserves that will almost certainly lose China money.
- Whatever the total aggregate demand consistent with low inflation, less excessive export growth leaves more room for satisfaction of the consumption needs of Chinese citizens.
- Chinese export industries are nearing the limits of market penetration by current products, largely assemblies, and need to move up the food chain to more sophisticated parts manufacture – a move that emphasises quality rather than quantity and is aided by the discipline of a higher exchange rate.

These industrial arguments will be outlined more fully below. But whatever the motivation, the government has spoken strongly against yuan appreciation. This may, and probably will, change over time, but current attitudes leave only the alternatives of accepting inflation and curbing domestic demand.

For a while acceptance of some inflation seems probable. The Chinese authorities retain the conviction that they can control inflation, and are thus likely to be complacent about it to start with. The problem is that the shift towards inflation is extremely rapid. Comparison with the US is apposite here. In America, overheating of 1% (GDP 1% above its long-term trend level) tends to produce a rise in the inflation rate of ¼% a year. Likewise, slack of 1% (GDP 1% below its long-term trend level) tends to lower the inflation rate by ¼% a year. So the current Chinese output gap of over 5–6%, strong overheating, would raise inflation by 1¼–1½% a year in the US. But in China the swing has been much more violent. From its low point of −1.8% in July 2009 (deflation) the CPI moved to 2.4% in March 2010. This is a huge 4.2% positive swing, despite many prices being controlled, notably energy costs. China's inflation appears much more sensitive to overheating (and slack) than America's, even though it is America that is regarded as the free-market centre of the world.

Commentators wishing to downplay Chinese inflation point out that it is concentrated in food. Food price inflation shifted from −1.2% in July 2009 (less intense deflation than the February 2009 low of −1.9%) to 5.2% in March, a 6.4 percentage point swing over the same eight months in which the total CPI shifted by 4.2%. But food prices are not non-core in China, in contrast to their treatment in the US. On the contrary, when migrant workers, laid off in the winter of 2008–09, got back to work again, the first thing they did was eat better. China remains a country of mostly poor people. Food is one-third of the CPI. It is the core. As people went back to work and wages went up, demand-pull inflation showed up first in food prices. In 2007, the acceleration of food prices, ahead of economic overheating, was very much a supply-side matter, pig disease being the primary cause. But in the late 2009 overheating, excess demand was the driver.

For veterans of the 1970s great inflation, there is that sure sign of an inflationary spiral: wage inflation. The economy swung by a lightning 8–9% vis-à-vis trend from 3% of slack in early 2009 to 5–6% overheating just three quarters later at the end of the year. Once the migrant workers had been taken on again, wage inflation soared to 20% or more. There is talk that this is a one-off, compensating for no increases the year before. But that is what people always say when a spiral is starting. In reality, wages are going up because labour is now scarce, and export industries are having too easy a time at the cheap exchange rate. If nothing is done, and inflation accelerates to reflect labour costs rising more than 10% faster than productivity, soaring inflation will ensure similar, maybe larger, wage increases in future.

The rapid shift to rising prices makes it likely that the government will continue to respond with monetary tightening – moderate to start with as inflation is not yet above the 3% target set for 2010 (down from the heavily undershot 4% target for 2009). In that case, the housing boom could start to be nipped in the bud by slower credit growth – and probably rising interest rates. The upswing of inflation could well take it to the 5–6% region by late 2010, causing the monetary tightening to be a classic too much, too late. In that case the disappointment of investors would come fairly quickly; in some cases, perhaps, before the building being bought has even been completed. The lightning advance could quickly relapse. But construction booms tend to have strong momentum of their own, so the policy tightening may have to be longer and tougher even than that suggested here.

These violent fluctuations of policy and markets in China have to be detrimental to good long-term growth. This is a general problem: massive policy responses to perceived problems cause huge movements that then require massive responses in the opposite direction. This induces extreme caution by businesses in respect of any actions that do not produce a large short-term pay-off. Such an outcome would not be so much a matter of a bubble bursting as Beijing policy imitating Milton Friedman's 'fool in the shower': swinging the dial to scalding when the water is a bit cold, only to be burned and swing the dial back to freezing – and thus never reaching a comfortable temperature.

In effect, the balance of China's policy is in the process of shifting massively from the beneficial stimulation of domestic demand to something closely resembling business as usual, circa 2005–07: export-led growth with a bit of overheating. On this analysis, the examination of policy to see whether the consumption rate might actually be stimulated above the recent 49% is no longer relevant, as the chief impact of China will take the form of a continued large net export surplus. Moreover, the mixture of an increasing Chinese share in now much less buoyant world trade and the further build-up of excessive industrial capacity means that Chinese expansion is likely to detract from business elsewhere, and be deflationary.

With a large trade and current-account surplus, and huge foreign-exchange reserves, China could logically conclude that restraining export demand is the best way forward – preserving as much as possible of the forward domestic-demand impetus from the late 2008 stimulus. To some extent this may be the outcome, as world trade could slow as the rebound generated by worldwide easing of inventory liquidation loses force, especially given the violent deflation being implemented in Europe.

The point about China's need for a rising exchange rate is partly a reflection of the country's sheer size. Its level of economic development is still consistent with a pure 'throw money at it' imitation approach to development. China's 2009 GDP was one-third of America's at current prices and exchange rates. Its population is four times larger, so that means an apparent per person GDP only one-twelfth of the size, some 8%. But if Chinese GDP is re-measured at purchasing-power parity (PPP) – that is, at US prices, not Chinese – this changes. GDP moves up to 60% of America's, and per person GDP to 14% (from 8%). Even at one-seventh of the US income level (14%), China ought to be able to pursue a pure catch-up policy of forced marches backed by technology transfer.

Chinese GDP is 12% of the world's at PPP, and close to half is manufacturing, so Chinese manufacturing, some 4–5% of world GDP, accounts for up to one-fifth of the world's. China's exports exceed those of the US, and even Germany, the former number one exporter. But its output is much less than those sales imply, as it is concentrated in the low-skilled, low-value, assembly end of industrial processes, with the high-value, sophisticated parts to be assembled still to a large degree sourced from Japan, South Korea and Taiwan. As a result, that one-fifth of world manufacturing value added amounts to a much higher proportion of world assembly activity, verging on global monopoly in many cases. But that means growth can proceed only at the pace of world markets, unless China can move back up the food chain into parts manufacture. So it is forced to move in this direction by its size much sooner than would be normal – at a much lower level of relative per person GDP.

What Japanese and German experience in the 1960s and 1970s demonstrated was that a rising real exchange rate is a good spur to greater sophistication – to the shift into higher-value products. When gaining export market share ceases to be easy, on the basis of cheap labour, firms have to start working harder to upgrade product quality, specifications and the type of product being produced. A higher relative cost of labour forces more efficient use of capital, which China is throwing at industry anyhow. Of course, China can, and in 2010 will, get a higher relative cost of labour by means of wage and price inflation, but that has great dangers – not least for the Communist Party government, whose power was much more threatened in past periods by inflation than by cyclical economic downswings. It is more effective by far to have moderate inflation and a rising nominal exchange rate.

Nonetheless, restraint of domestic demand is the likely main course in 2010. Some restraint is unavoidable whatever is done on the exchange-rate front. Money and credit need to be growing at 15% or less – less than half their gain during 2009. The governor of the People's Bank of China, Zhou Xiaochuan, has signalled the likelihood of measures to withdraw liquidity and raise interest rates. This means in effect that the orders have already gone out to China's largely state-owned banks. During 2009, China's credit and broad money expansion was the only source of major monetary growth in the world. That is about to be seriously curtailed. In pursuing this course while protecting exporters from any restraint, China is conforming to the global pattern of reverting to type – just as the US reverts to debt-induced expansion.

Apart from the need to move up more quickly from mere assembly to sophisticated products, the other threat to the sustenance of China's growth momentum comes from its mercantilist obsession with exports. Like Japan before it, China could suffer a slowdown in growth if it does not shift towards a consumer-oriented, market-price domestic economy. In Japan, the shift from premium growth (an average of 4½% a year in the 1980s) to near-stagnation (1% at best ever since) occurred as its bubble burst in 1990. That bubble had involved excessive, debt-driven investment just as China has experienced recently. When it burst, Japan's top-down, directed system of development failed to adjust to spurring rapid growth of the domestic consumer market. The inability of a directed system to use market-price signals to move resources into activities and sectors of comparative advantage meant the drop in growth rates was driven as much by supply-side failures as demand-side issues.

China needs policies to raise the long-run tendency to consume and lower the desire to save – on a massive scale. Consumption (household and government) is now under 49% of GDP. What does it need to rise to? This question can best be answered by reference to desirable or natural levels for the other demand components of GDP. For fixed investment, analysis of capital/output ratios and needed returns on capital (ROC) suggests that a 10% real growth rate and adequate ROC imply an investment rate of 33–35% of GDP. But future Chinese growth is highly unlikely to reach the past trend rate of 10%. So an investment rate of 30% of GDP should be enough, with 33% the upper limit. The net exports surplus that seems indicated by the vulnerability of demand in the rest of the world is well below the recent 7–10% of GDP: 3–5% seems the most that should prudently be relied on. Add in 1–2%

for inventory building, and the total for non-consumption items adds up to 34–40%, 37% being the mid-point of this range. But this requires consumption to be raised by a huge 14 percentage points, from the recent 49% to 63% of GDP.

Policies to achieve this could include the following:

- housing and mortgage loan stimulus/subsidy;
- establishment of social security;
- establishment of full freehold title to land and real estate;
- abolition of controls on exports of capital.

The quickest stimulus probably lies in housing. Housing is effective as a means of generating demand as it involves not only the construction of buildings, but also major household expenditure on furnishing, decoration, household equipment, and so on. This is the measure that the government should develop for the medium term, holding onto recent momentum. While housing development entails infrastructure spending to back it up, a public investment programme oriented to support a housing boom induced by mortgage and other tax/expenditure subsidies seems the best immediate route to raising the proportion of household spending in China. To minimise the danger from a new bubble, permanent subsidies directed at poorer families are needed, as the scope for people to afford more housing is limited by their income. Moreover, the willingness of the Chinese to mimic their American cousins and lower savings in a housing boom could be held back by broader social insecurity.

In the West, the mantra 'don't lose your job, don't lose your health, and don't grow old' has been mitigated since 1950 by social security systems and private financial products, providing people with security against unemployment, illness and retirement. China has yet to establish nearly enough of such systems, through either government provisions (social security) or privately provided financial products (health insurance, private pensions, life assurance, and so on). Given the government's overarching goal of retaining political power and control, social security is a natural area of development for policies to encourage consumption. Parallel financial products in the private sector would be consistent with the policy of developing a modern financial system, and also with the need for rapid growth of the mortgage market. Even if pursued as a priority, however, this is a ten-year, rather than a two-year, project. Chinese economy optimists, who hope for consumption growth to emerge quickly, may well be disappointed by the pace of development of personal financial security.

When it comes to freehold title to land and real estate, little can be expected. Yet reforms could rapidly improve the economy in an area of high priority to the authorities: rural income growth. At the moment farmers have leases on their land – long ones, to be sure, of 30–40 years – but no ability to merge securely with neighbours in pursuit of mutual benefit, for example in irrigation or land use. Regional and local governments have not abandoned their habit of simply taking land when they need it, for example for a steel plant. With nearly half the population still on the land, this is an area where major advances in productivity, income and spending could be generated – but probably will not be, given the Communist Party's priority of control over people's lives and freedom for short-term policy action.

Another way to stimulate more consumption could be removal of capital export controls. Under current rules, the huge flow of

Chinese saving has to be invested almost entirely within China: the net export surplus and net capital outflows emerge via accumulation of foreign-exchange reserves by the People's Bank of China (PBOC). Investors have a choice between costly housing, low rates of interest on state-owned bank deposits and violently fluctuating stocks. These limited and risky options make for a high rate of saving, as existing wealth is insecure. In 2007, a PBOC unit, the State Administration for Foreign Exchange, proposed easing of controls on capital exports, but this was aborted. It has now been reinstated, but the attractions of stockmarket investment have been heavily qualified by the financial crisis. Nevertheless, it is a sensible time for Chinese people to export capital and obtain both higher returns and less volatility. In 2007, they would have been investing at the top of the market, but now they would be getting better value. A major outflow of savings onto world markets and resultant fall in the savings rate is unlikely within a 2–3 year time frame, however.

Ironically, removing capital export controls might help with the government's goal of holding down the yuan. In the current moderate global recovery, the struggle for export market share among savings-glut countries and protests from labour interests in the US are likely to get more intense. Nobody can refute the government's manipulation of China's currency, a prime point of (so far) rhetorical dispute. But if it were to abandon capital export controls, the flow of private investment funds out of the country might start to offset the net export surplus, weakening upward pressure on the yuan and permitting a badly needed float of the exchange rate. China would retain a degree of competitiveness without manipulation – the policy ideal. The tough conditions of the post-crisis world could make the next phase of

Chinese growth much less easy. A policy that might both keep the exchange rate down and promote a lower personal savings rate has strong attractions.

China's emphasis on excessive infrastructure and muscle-bound heavy industry aimed at exports has the capacity to create a similar supply-side inhibition to growth rates – though at a higher level – as in 1990s Japan. And a communist government focused on control more than on human welfare may be more likely than Japan's to fail to see the importance of consumer demand growth as a spur to profitable long-run growth. As the world increasingly resembles a globalised Japan, with the paradoxical mix of persistent huge government deficits and deflation, the other Japanese feature, slower growth, is also likely to be part of the mix. The danger is that China suffers the worst of this last, slow-growth part of the nasty cocktail. China even resembles Japan in that much of its excess saving arises from too great a concentration of income in the business sector, where it is often wastefully deployed, or effectively provides the deposits that underpin the build-up of foreign-exchange reserves, on which China makes regular, large losses. With the rest of the world likely to lower the boom on Chinese exports in one form or another quite soon, the government's response to these challenges could prove crucial to China's economic future.

The needed switch from excessive exports and investment to greater consumption is not merely a matter of changing policies, though that is a major hurdle in itself. The response pattern of the Chinese economy is built around current habits. Exports and investment are primary sources of demand (in contrast to the US, where it is consumption and net exports, with business spending in the secondary, responsive position). Consumption in China is responsive and secondary as it depends on growth of wage income deriving from the other two. To downsize the importance of exports and investment is likely to mean a dousing of consumption, not the desired substitution of greater consumer spending as a primary source of demand. Changing such habits requires determination, consistency and time. At best it will happen slowly; more probably, the switch will be only partial. In either case, China's growth trend in future years could be well down from the past 10%.

6

US growth held back, heading into deflation

The US recovery since spring 2009 has been driven by four factors:

- a snap-back of inventories from heavy liquidation to modest accumulation;
- import substitution and net export gains arising from structural factors and devaluation of the dollar;
- continued debt growth – given the excessive private-sector debts already accumulated, government borrowing and spending is now the source of debt stimulus;
- stockmarket recovery and house prices ceasing to fall, leading to the incipient rise in household savings during the recession to be largely reversed.

Real GDP in the first quarter of 2010 was 2.7% higher than the recession nadir three quarters earlier (the second quarter of 2009), a 3.6% annual rate of growth. The chief contributors to this 2¾% were 1½% each from real consumer spending and the inventory snap-back, plus 1¼% from exports, less a 1½% deduction for increased imports. The jump in imports was exaggerated by the inventory snap-back: imports are extremely sensitive to shifts in inventories. Excluding this factor, net exports (exports minus imports) made a small positive contribution to GDP growth, not the negative one derived from netting the raw numbers.

An unexpected feature of this recovery (for most commentators) is the recovery of real consumer spending. Its increase of 1½% over three quarters comes in spite of a ¾% fall in real personal disposable income. The savings rate – as a percentage of disposable income, not GDP – fell from 5.4% to 3.1%, accounting for the rise in spending. Its contribution was larger than that of the inventory snap-back, once the import intensity of the latter is netted out. By contrast, the contribution of government deficit budgeting was largely finished by the second quarter of 2009 – it peaked as the recession was at its worst, conforming to ideal anti-cyclical Keynesian policy. Whereas real government spending rose a little after the second quarter of 2009, the tax rebates peaked then, accounting in part for the high personal savings rate: households saved what were seen as one-off tax concessions. The shift into state and local government budget crisis as the recession took its toll on their tax revenues and relief spending has led real government spending to fall back in late 2009 and early 2010, so that its contribution to growth over the three quarters of recovery is roughly nil.

This brief outline already suggests that the recovery is unsound. What the US needs is growth led by net exports, so that domestic spending can grow more slowly than domestic incomes, reflecting an increase in net saving. And the gain in net saving needs to be in households, not business, as it is household debt that is structurally out of line; business debt is more in need of a cyclical downward adjustment that could anyhow be achieved by equity issuance rather than a major surge in saving. In the recovery so far, however, household net saving has hardly adjusted at all, import substitution has not stopped the revival of imports, driven by inventories, offsetting a good period for US exports, and the government's huge swing into deficit has found its counterpart in business net saving, which partly reflects strong profitability, but to a large extent cuts in fixed investment.

To understand the forces at work, and help analyse how the economy may develop in future, the Table 2 shows the US financial flows in 2006, the year when the private financial deficit was largest, 2008 Q1, on the eve of recession, and 2010 Q1, the latest quarter.

Table 2 **US flows of funds (conceptual basis), % of GDP**

	2006	2008 Q1[a]	2010 Q1
Household savings	1¾%	1%	2¼%
Housing investment	5¾%	−3½%	2½%
Household net flow	−4%	−2½%	−¼%
Business net flow[b]	¼%	2%	6¾%
Private sector (sum above)	−3¾%	−½%	6½%
Government	−2¼%	−4½%	−10%
Foreign[c]	6%	5%	3½%

a High point for real GDP before recession.
b Treated as a residual, given measurement of the other items.
c Equals current-account balance with sign reversed.

The salient points from Table 2 are that the business financial surplus accounts more than fully for the private surplus, which itself accounts for two-thirds of the government deficit (10% of GDP), the other one-third being the current-account deficit (foreigners' surplus in Table 2). The business surplus was actually somewhat larger in 2009 Q2–Q4, as inventory liquidation was intense. But inventory behaviour was back to normal (modest accumulation) by early 2010, so the latest net business financial position accurately represents the underlying current position.

As observed in Chapter 4, getting the business surpluses to finance the deficits is not straightforward. Normal, non-bank businesses do not generally hold government bonds, so these surpluses may partly be used for debt pay-down – releasing the previous investors in such debt to buy government debt instead – but partly goes abroad or into stock buybacks, bids, and so on. This has helped the stockmarket recovery, which has been the sharpest in history, and in turn encouraged complacency in households. Partly as a result, the latter have saved less and spent more, as described above, helping the recovery but postponing adjustment to the higher savings that will over time be necessary.

The basic point to be argued here is that the US personal savings rate needs to rise to 7–8% of disposable income, or 5–6% of GDP. With housing perhaps recovering to 3% of GDP, this would create a positive household financial balance (as in Table 2) of 2–3% of GDP. Such an increase in household saving would clearly cut demand, so that gains in net exports are crucial to healthy recovery – that is, both growth and financial adjustment. Even a drastic shift such as elimination of the US current-account deficit would still leave a government deficit of 4–5% of GDP if the business financial surplus were cut by two-thirds to 2% of GDP. (In Table 2, the private surplus would be 4–5% of GDP, 2–3% in households and 2% in business.) Yet a cut of two-thirds in the business surplus would be unlikely to be entirely caused by greater fixed capital spending, despite implicitly buoyant net exports, with consumer spending only growing slowly. So some erosion of profit margins is implied. This means that to get the government deficit down to acceptable levels (maximum 3% of GDP – see Chapter 9), and sustain good business profitability while holding down domestic consumer demand as savings increase, could require the current account to shift to significant surplus. That this is unlikely to happen, given trends in the rest of the world, means the US has an unpleasant choice between below-trend growth and failing to reduce financial imbalances. The likely outcome, as analysed here, could be a bit of both.

After leading rapid fourth quarter growth in 2009, inventories are likely to make only a minor contribution to growth during 2010. The inventory/sales ratio in early 2010 was 1.27, still above its pre-recession low point of 1.25, and above the long-run trend for this ratio, which (helped by high-tech capital management) is declining over time. With negligible inflation, half a year's growth at or above the long-run trend rate of 2½% would be required to bring the ratio to sales back to its long-run trend, without any addition of new inventory. So the modestly positive inventory accumulation in the first quarter of 2010 is unlikely to be much exceeded any time over the next year or more, as the ratio to sales could remain above its desired level. As a growth factor, inventories seem exhausted.

What about net export prospects? This breaks down into export growth and import substitution. The wave of import substitution since 2006, representing improved US net exports, has shifted gear to growth of exports recently. This suggests it does not just reflect special factors and may represent improved competitiveness of US business over and above the relative-cost benefit of the weak dollar. The volume of imports started down in summer 2007, three-quarters ahead of real GDP. Over the subsequent ten quarters imports have fallen a net 12%, compared with

½% for real GDP. Some of this reflects a gathering response to the high price of oil, which has fallen in usage by 12% to 18½ million barrels per day (mbpd), with extra US production further shrinking imports, which are down about one-quarter at 10 mbpd. Another part of the story is that car sales were particularly hard hit in the recession, and these are import-intensive compared to the rest of the economy.

A major factor is the improved relative performance of US business, aided by the cheaper dollar. Better productivity growth – relative to both past performance and other advanced nations – is a major favourable factor for the US economy over the medium term. Productivity growth measured by the 7½-year average that eliminates most cyclical effects, has recently accelerated above 2½% a year. Normally in recessions it suffers – badly therefore in severe recessions – but not this time. On the contrary, the recession has been so severe in part because US firms have slashed payrolls, inventory and capital spending faster than they have lost sales – a virtuous circle at the expense of importers. While imports are bound to rise even in a modest recovery like this one, the competitiveness of US business should continue to keep this in check. But whereas it was reinforced in 2009 by the decline of the dollar (as well as oil and car import cuts), this is ceasing to be the case as the dollar appreciates. So the import substitution effect could prove only moderate in future.

When it comes to exports, as with inventories and import substitution, the best may already be past. Exports grew fast in the last two quarters of 2009, but slowed in the first quarter of 2010. This slowing could continue. Chinese demand has been the single largest contributor to world recovery over the past year, leading to an overheated Chinese economy. This has boosted commodity countries in particular, helping important US markets in the Americas, notably Canada and Brazil. The impending Chinese tightening should deflate metal and energy prices, though perhaps not agricultural commodities. Export buoyancy to commodity countries is probably over. Meanwhile, the total shambles in Europe (see Chapter 7), together with dollar appreciation against the euro and probably the pound, is likely to hit US exports in that other major market for the US.

The chief weakness of the recovery is that the US economy seems able to grow only with demand stimulated by credit, credit and yet more credit. With households and business above their debt capacity, government debt is now being piled up instead. In the ten years to 1997, for every $1 of extra nominal GDP, the US saw the sum of household, non-financial business and government debt increase by $3.30. The comparative number for the 1950s–70s was $1.30, and even at the height of Reaganomic high leverage that number was about $2½. Now, to get a growth rate over the six quarters to the end of 2010 of at most 3%, more probably 2%, with minimal inflation, the government (including state and local) is having to borrow an extra 10% of GDP. There is an offset from net pay-down of private-sector debt, but aggregate debt could still increase faster than GDP. So the US is engaged in debt-heavy growth as usual, but starting from much worse ratios than before.

The one-third of the government deficit that is accounted for by the current-account deficit is likely to shrink only gradually, as we have seen. The two-thirds that is matched by business financial surplus has mostly merely offset the slashing of business spending in the recession; as such the budget deficit has protected the economy against an even more vicious decline, rather than acting as a recovery agent. Nor is business investment likely to expand rapidly now that the inventory snap-back has matured. Certainly, the level of business capital spending is not far above the replacement level – that is, depreciation – but it does not need to be. Capacity utilisation in industry is still one-tenth below its long-run norm. Underutilised capacity abounds in service sectors too. The sheer strength of business cash flow is likely to cause some growth of business capital spending, but its profitability depends on extra demand, which is limited – and hence, likewise, the rebound of such business spending is likely to be limited. The same is true of housing investment, given the overhang of surplus supply (see Chapter 2).

So the scope for short-term cuts in the government deficit could be limited – without hitting growth – even before allowing for any increase in household saving, which would tend to swell further the private financial surplus. The deficit should be reduced a little during 2010 as the recovery to date has been above expectations owing to falling personal saving. But substantial and multi-year progress to what is viewed as a sustainable deficit level, perhaps 3% of GDP, seems improbable at present.

It seems self-evident that there must be some limit to growth that depends on an ever-rising ratio of debt to income. Yet the US economy seems to know no other way of growing. In the private sector, the limits are reasonably clear. Increased debt will depend on rising asset values, to secure the debt, and asset values can rise relative to income only by lowering the return on assets. Hence the connection with bubbles. But at some stage financial markets blow the whistle (or in Chuck Prince parlance, 'the music stops') and asset prices fall back under their own weight – bubbles burst, in other words. The debt ceases to be bearable, and the economy recedes. This is roughly what happened in 2007–09.

Are there similar limits on a government debt run-up? It is tempting to say there are not, with interest rates nil, or at least very low, and a cram-down investor called China compelled by its currency peg to the dollar to pick up the tab. Nobody expects the government to repay its debt – its ratio to GDP/income may come down eventually, but that will probably reflect rising income (either real or, less likely, through inflation) rather than debt repayment. So the talk of burdens on future generations is a bit abstract. They, after all, will be the chief beneficiaries of rising income. The true burden can be represented as the interest payments, and that seems quite small right now. (See Chapter 9 for a full analysis of the government debt problem.)

It is one thing to say that current levels of borrowing and spending may not have to be withdrawn in the near future for precautionary reasons, but quite another to suggest that this creates a buoyant prospect for US growth. The problem is that in principle, a continued budget deficit at any particular level (in this case 10% of GDP) does not create extra stimulus – it is the original move up to that level that is the stimulus. For the most part a sustained budget deficit, even at a high level, is neutral for growth.

As a modest recovery proceeds, and some reduction of the budget deficit will occur cyclically, as tax revenues recover, this effect is likely to be augmented by deliberate policy tightening – at the state and local level at least. Most states and localities have balanced-budget laws to comply with, as well as natural debt constraints. These operate with a lag, so that the collapse of tax revenues in the recession will lead to cuts in spending or increased taxes during 2010. It is by no means clear that California, Illinois, New York and New Jersey will not provide at least one Greece within the US. Moreover, the recent political

Figure 18   **US household net wealth and savings rate**

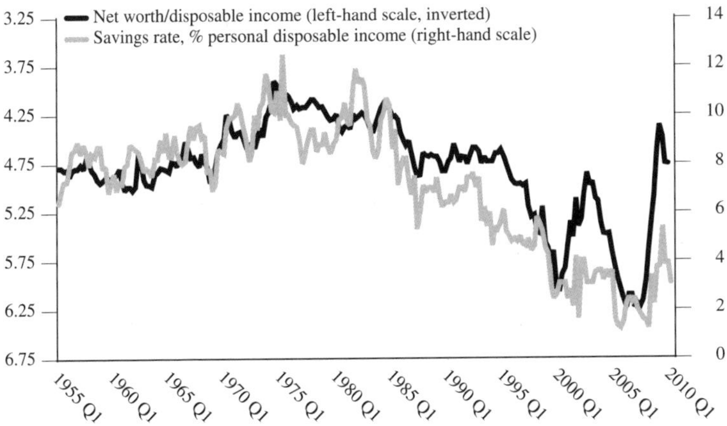

Sources: US Fed; BEA

trends against the Democrats – the so-called 'tea parties' – may prove to have created a major political impetus towards budget retrenchment at the federal level too. So for the purposes of economic development over the 12–24 month term we can conclude that rising government debt may not enforce deflation of federal budget deficits, but that fiscal policy will nonetheless be tightened, and act as a drag on the economy.

The other negative aspect of the debt situation is the increased need for personal saving to repay excessive household debts and to build up assets in the face of the collapse of existing asset values. Figure 18 shows how net household assets peaked at 6¼ times disposable income 2½ years ago, and bottomed out at 4¼ times in the first quarter of 2009. The significant recovery of stockmarkets and stabilisation of house prices since then only took this ratio up to a little under 4¾ times. Past relationships of personal savings to net assets suggest this wealth level, which is unlikely to improve much from now on, is consistent with a savings rate of 7–8% of disposable income, compared with the recent rate of 3%. If such a shift upwards of more than four percentage points in the savings rate were to occur in one year, it would probably mean falling real consumer spending, as real disposable income is highly unlikely to rise by over 4%. More likely, the adjustment will be slower than that. But this still represents a formidable headwind for the economy over the next few years.

Siren voices in America are expressing the hope that this household savings behaviour adjustment will not happen; that apparently booming asset values and very low interest rates will encourage households to put off debt repayment and accumulation of assets. Aside from the longer-term damage this would do, it is improbable, as asset values are likely to stabilise, if not wilt, in the face of much tougher conditions over the next 6–12 months than recently. The obvious point is that the benefit from quantitative easing (QE) is about to go away, as it ended in the first quarter of 2010. This has already helped drive the major recent upswing of long-term bond yields. Moreover, the euro-crisis has boosted the dollar, damaging America's internationally diversified major firms' profits.

If US markets, or the economy, continue the above-trend growth of the past three quarters, the Fed could soon start to unwind its quantitative easing – selling mortgage-backed securities and others into the market to shrink its currently artificially swollen balance sheet. The deeper, more powerful point against further stockmarket gains is that the chief source of actual liquidity growth in the world, China, is about to be forced to tighten monetary policy significantly. Chinese stocks are clearly past their peak and well down, and their cycle led the world on the upside when recovery started in winter 2008–09.

A rogue factor in assessing US prospects is population trends. The ageing of baby-boomers means that the first wave – those born in 1946 – reach 65 in 2011. This is unlikely to be their retirement age, however. These people have not saved much. They have seen house prices drop by 35% or so, preventing an alternative strategy of downsizing their homes to release capital to fund a pension. Many, perhaps most, will have to stay at work. This will cut into the job prospects of younger people, who could well suffer sustained unemployment. In effect, baby-boomers not retiring will cause an increase in the US labour force above that arising from the (slow) growth of the conventional working-age population (that is, aged 16–64) plus net immigration. This is a modest plus factor for demand (see below) and a substantial plus factor for supply. As such it will put fresh downward pressure on both price and labour-cost inflation, and will intensify US competitive pressure on the rest of the world.

The non-retiring baby-boomers, still in work and increasingly conscious of financial vulnerability as they age, are likely to save their social-security cheques. Hence the likelihood of increased output and income, with more saving and less spending, driving the economy away from net imports towards overseas payments equilibrium. Whether through modestly restrictive fiscal policy action, withdrawal of the Fed's QE, or baby-boomer behaviour, or all of the above, savings rates will probably increase in the medium term. Overall prospects are for growth falling back to its trend rate of around 2½% during 2010, and possibly undershooting that trend rate over 2011–12. One result is that slack in the economy should remain more than 5%, and deflation could emerge.

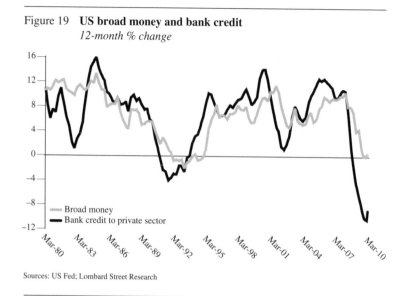

Figure 19 **US broad money and bank credit**
12-month % change

Sources: US Fed; Lombard Street Research

Bank lending to the private sector has shrunk by 9–10% in the past 12 months. Although private-sector debt is not falling this fast, the banks' share of it is being cut by strong public-market bond issuance. An increase in banks' holdings of government paper, together with dollar-carry loans to foreigners funding assets and derivatives with cheap dollars, has been essential for broad money growth at all; without it, the shrinkage of private loans would have been largely reflected in broad money. As it is, by helping fund the budget deficit, and buying Fed paper issued under its quantitative easing programme, the banks have expanded their balance sheets a little, and 12-month broad money growth is under 1%.

This is the lowest broad-money growth rate since the jobless recovery of the early 1990s, when the perceived bankruptcy of Citibank and others caused the lending business to migrate to the public money and bond markets. In a country habituated to debt growing faster than GDP, negligible broad-money growth should slow the economy over time. More immediately, fuel for the risk-asset rally is being removed. Both the deflationary economic effect and the credit impact will be reinforced by Chinese tightening (see Chapter 5). US monetary growth of 1% exactly equals that of the Big Four developed economies – the US, the euro zone, Japan and Britain – combined. Take away rapid Chinese monetary growth and world liquidity will be severely squeezed. Neither in the US nor internationally can risk assets be expected to avoid deflationary ripples spreading from the Pacific rim.

For most sincere monetarists, these monetary trends are enough by themselves to make talk of rising inflation highly implausible. But such talk persists, because of a confusion between printing money (the Fed's QE, which has been large) and broad money growth (the chief driver of inflation under Friedmanite monetary theory). Inflationistas aspiring to sophistication sometimes talk of a 'rise in velocity' (or circulation of money) causing inflation, even without strong monetary growth. But velocity of circulation is simply GDP divided by money supply. If it rises, either GDP is going up or money is going down (or both). If money supply is going down, the chances of accelerating inflation are small, so it is only GDP going up that we have to worry about. So rising velocity is simply an obscure way of saying 'rapid GDP growth'.

Nobody ever disputed the idea that rapid GDP growth leading to overheating would cause faster inflation (as it already has in China). The question is precisely that: will GDP grow fast enough to cause overheating? The Friedmanite approach is to regard the output gap, the deviation of real GDP from its trend, as the measure of overheating or slack. Although Lombard Street

Figure 20 **US hourly labour cost change**
% per year

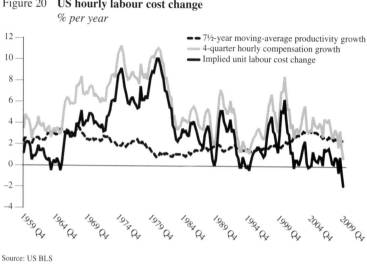

Legend:
- 7½-year moving-average productivity growth
- 4-quarter hourly compensation growth
- Implied unit labour cost change

Source: US BLS

Research's estimate of trend growth has fallen well below the long-run average GDP growth range of 3–3¼% since 2002, and is now down to 2¼%, we still find that actual GDP was 5½% below the trend level in early 2010. It is likely to remain negative by 5% or more throughout 2010, and again in 2011–12, given the growth prospects described above. The relationship of inflation to the output gap in the past has been that a 1% gap produces a ¼% change in the inflation rate.

With the output gap moving from positive to negative in early 2008, and then plunging to –7% at its worst, core inflation (somewhat lagged) fell from a peak of 2.7% in summer 2008 to the recent 0.9%. If growth is modest in the first year or two of recovery, and the slack in the economy remains in the 5–6% region, inflation should be cut by 1¼–1½% each year, meaning it will be nil by late 2010 or early 2011, and then negative – probably for several years, as it could take that long to eliminate all the slack in the economy. Clearly, these kind of statistical relationships may not hold at ultra-low rates of inflation. But on Friedmanite logic, the chances of rising inflation are nil and of falling prices very high.

Some analysts prefer to look at the unemployment rate, and consider wage inflation as the chief driver of inflation. Calculations of the NAIRU – the clumsily named non-accelerating-inflation rate of unemployment – have put it at around 5½–5¾% in the US. By this reckoning, even if some of the recent surge in unemployment reflects jobs that will never come back, its rise to 10% is virtually a guarantor of falling inflation, probably deflation itself. Already the rate of gain of US hourly pay has fallen below the productivity growth trend, meaning output per hour goes up faster than hourly pay so that labour costs per unit of output are falling. This is not particularly surprising, with unemployment at 10%. In all probability, hourly pay growth will fall further and unit labour costs will soon be falling fast, to be followed by consumer prices themselves.

In Chapter 9 the government debt problem is analysed in an international context, beginning with Japan, and the conclusion is that US net government debt will rise for another five years to reach 90–100% of GDP, compared with 56% at the end of 2009. The danger is that if the US continues at that time to have a current-account deficit, and private-sector balance sheets and financial flows have been adjusted to a sustainable basis, the net government debt burden could continue to rise after that. A stable government debt level could depend on the current account returning to balance or even surplus, as the long-run equilibrium rate of private-sector financial balance is a surplus of some 3% of

GDP, and it is likely to be higher than this for the next few years, as described above. So the government deficit needs to equal that is 3% of GDP even with no current-account deficit. And in a non-inflationary world, a 3% budget deficit and 3% real growth would imply a 100% net debt ratio staying unchanged. With a current-account deficit and 3% private surpluses, the budget deficit would be larger and the net debt ratio probably rising from 100%.

Just as China has reverted to old habits in the form of export-led growth, the US continues to depend for growth on increasing debt relative to GDP, this time government debt. Given the pivotal role of the current-account balance in future prospects, and the threat of future budget disequilibrium from health and welfare costs as the baby-boomers retire and age, the danger is that US law-makers fall back on direct protectionism from free trade to permit domestic stability. Sadly, this would create more problems than solutions. The chief danger would be the loss of real income from a less optimal reflection of comparative advantage as trade flows are distorted. But foreign retaliation would also harm the US, as would the loss of net overseas income as the world economy could only be seriously damaged.

7

The euro-catastrophe

Euro-imbalances worsen, threaten crisis

It was former Chancellor Helmut Kohl of Germany whose over-weening self-assurance caused him to plunge on from the necessary and desirable unification of Germany to the highly risky Economic and Monetary Union (EMU) within the European Union. The decisive error of allowing Italy and then Greece into EMU is now starting to show its full malignant consequences. And the inclusion of fast-growth, then relatively low-income, Spain and Ireland created temptations for excessively debt-driven development that has proved a primrose path to the edge of ruin. The Maastricht criteria for participating in EMU were designed to exclude Italy. Italy never came close to meeting all the criteria, and one major test it did pass was on the basis of fiddled budget statistics. Much the same was true of Greece. Their admission to EMU was a purely political decision – and blunder.

Europe has three economic disaster zones and deficit-ridden Britain:

- The south (Mediterranean Europe). Italy, Spain, Portugal and Greece are all in severe supply-side collapse, with massive overvaluation within the euro, as well as suffering from debt/deficit problems.

- The east (central and eastern Europe and points east and south-east). These economies are suffering from gross excess debts and collapsing export markets in western Europe, but they retain both the vulnerability and policy flexibility of non-membership of the euro.

- The north-central (Germany, Benelux, Nordic countries, Switzerland and Austria). These economies are highly competitive, but have domestic savings rates that exceed investment in full employment conditions by 7–8% of GDP, so in a demand-deficient world their dependence on exports has led to a collapse of output and income.

- The Atlantic isles (Britain and Ireland). As these two economies have far exceeded their credit limits, they do not have the freedom to run up government borrowing to the full, modern ideal of 'on-trend growth with low inflation', as their ability to borrow the money is compromised by existing excessive indebtedness.

The driving influence of the Eurasian savings glut is described in Chapter 2 (and in Appendix 2). In Europe, as in the trans-Pacific US/Pacific-Asian imbalances, fixed exchange rates were and are a key factor. The New Dollar Area (NDA) concept of my Lombard Street Research colleague, Brian Reading, in August 2004 contributed to the origination of the savings-glut idea in September of that year. The NDA was based on China's then-fixed yuan peg to the US dollar, and the soft pegs of various other Pacific Asian savings-glutton currencies to the dollar (to avoid too much hollowing out by the feared Chinese). The comparable imbalances within Europe were encouraged and have been made more damaging by fixed rates in EMU, as also described in Chapter 2.

Club Med and Ireland: sick men of Europe

The four Mediterranean countries and Ireland are the troubled periphery of the euro zone. Two types of economic affliction threaten them with prolonged stagnation and financial instability. The first is simple overvaluation of costs and prices. Where labour costs or prices have risen substantially more than for Germany, France and Benelux (the euro-zone core), the normal remedy would be devaluation and tight monetary and/or fiscal policy. This is not available within EMU, so the result tends to be tight policy but without the release into competitiveness and net export growth via devaluation: net export gains are liable to consist entirely of reduced imports through slow growth, stagnation or recession. Restoration of labour-cost competitiveness requires ultra-high unemployment to drive down wages relative to those of, say, Germany, which are themselves heavily repressed.

The second affliction is excessive deficits, and sometimes debts, in countries that have grown extremely rapidly through the benefit of interest rates kept artificially low by the euro zone averaging process – essentially 'one size fits none'. The fast-growth countries have benefited as rates were set mostly by reference to the needs of the slow-growth, low-inflation core countries. Spain is the country that comes in both groups: overvalued and, until the crisis, fast-growth. Italy and Portugal are grossly overvalued, and, partly as a result, have not even enjoyed fast growth – or any growth at all in Italy's case. Ireland and Greece are not seriously overvalued, but they have generated huge external deficits owing to fast growth and now have dangerously large government deficits. These last two are not overvalued in cost terms at least

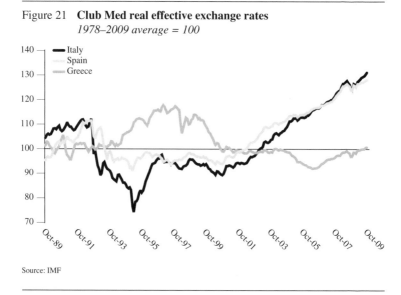

Figure 21   **Club Med real effective exchange rates**
1978–2009 average = 100

Source: IMF

partly because they have enjoyed fairly good growth in productivity since EMU started, unlike the other three.

Within the euro context, the only remedy for these countries is deflation, but Ireland is the only one of these peripheral invalids that has effectively accepted this and taken its medicine. Recently, Greece's hand has been forced by financial crisis and rapid escalation of borrowing costs – as well as peer-pressure from the euro-zone core, which is having to bail it out. The prospects for Italy and Spain are, at best, grim stagnation for the medium term.

Italian competitiveness irretrievable within EMU
Figure 21 shows the relative labour-cost competitiveness of peripheral EMU countries, as calculated by the IMF (adjusting nominal effective exchange rates for relative unit labour cost changes). The late 1980s and early 1990s were the high-corruption-boom

period in Italy. This collapsed in 1992–93, and with it the Christian Democratic Party that had ruled Italy since the second world war. Some reconstitution of political order in the mid-1990s enabled the lira to settle down and go into the euro at 95% of the 30-year average; this 95 level looks like the right rate for Italy. On this basis, with the index now at 130, Italian labour costs are some 30–35% overvalued.

Italian overvaluation almost exactly equals that of Germany at the peak of the post-unification upsurge. But (not by coincidence) that peak in 1995 was also the high point of the deutschmark (DM) after the ERM shake-out of 1992–93 (with even France allowed a temporary 15% downward adjustment). The fall of the German real rate from around 130 to around 105 in 2001 almost exactly reflected the fall of the nominal effective exchange rate. In other words, it was not caused by any special restraint of labour costs. In 1995–98 the DM fell sharply vis-à-vis other currencies, as did the euro itself from its inception in January 1999 until autumn 2000. Only from 2002–05 onwards did labour cost cuts contribute much to Germany's gains in competitiveness, when the rise in the euro was offset by falling wages and rapidly falling unit labour costs. Even then, however, Germany's relative cost improvement mostly consisted of not sharing the cost inflation of the other EMU members, including Italy.

For Italy, this means that the chief period of German adjustment, 1996–2001, is no precedent, unless the euro crashes. And the crash would have to be extreme, as euro weakness would not benefit Italy's costs vis-à-vis other EMU members. For example, a one-third fall of the euro against the dollar from autumn 2009's $1.50 to $1.00 would cut Italy's trade-weighted exchange rate by only 10–12%. Let us suppose that the unit labour costs of Italy's trading partners rise at 1% a year for ten years. Then to get Italy's real effective rate back to 95 in Figure 21 would require its unit labour costs to fall by up to 2% a year. But Italian productivity gains are zero to negative. So wages would have to fall at 2% a year for ten years. Yet their increase in the past decade has been 2½–3% a year. In any normal view of the euro's future exchange rate, the unemployment needed to get labour costs competitive will be pure sadism, and ensure nil growth for a full decade, and probably outright long-run falls in real income. (Already, Italy's real GDP is <u>lower</u> than at the end of the 2001 recession: nil growth over eight years.) Moreover, in the current deflationary state of the world Italy's trading partners' labour costs could well not rise at all, making the required drop in Italian wages that much more severe.

Mired Italian productivity: stagnation for a decade

EMU-enthusiasts who blame Italy's problems on the supply side have a perfectly good point – but only a partial point. However badly Italy's supply-side problems may affect prospective real income, the forthcoming grim adjustments will be made that much more – and unnecessarily more – painful by the absence of an exchange-rate salve. On many bases of analysis, productivity is actually falling in Italy. Figure 22 shows value added per worker in Italian industry and services over the past 15 years. While it has only gradually fallen in services, in industry it has moved sideways, and then recently lapsed badly.

Since the end of the earlier, 2001 recession, Italy (and Germany) went through a long near-stagnation until early 2005, and then a relatively short upswing until early 2008. By then Italian real GDP was up nearly 7% from the fourth quarter of

Figure 22 **Italy: output/worker**
2000 = 100

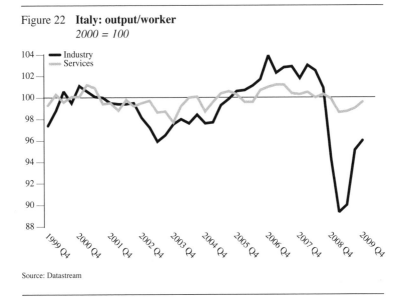

Source: Datastream

2001, somewhat over 1% a year on average. But the subsequent recession means it is now below its eight-year earlier level. Such a full-cycle decline in real GDP is a first for a major economy in the period since the second world war.

What are the supply-side elements of this prospective stagnation? A short list would include:

- absence of the rule of law;
- focus on commodity products after decades of dependence on devaluations;
- extreme weakness in high technology;
- primitive financial system and mortgage market;
- numerous petty legal obstacles to optimal distribution of resources.

Absence of the rule of law – results from court action, if at

Figure 23 **Real GDP since end of last recession**
2001 Q4 = 100

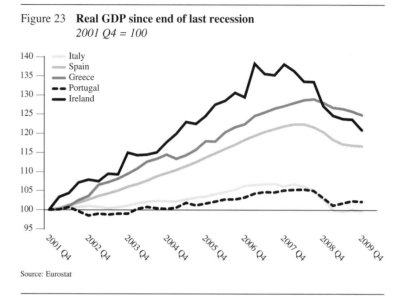

Source: Eurostat

all possible, take years, even decades – means Italian firms need alternative methods of resolving disputes. This makes for family firms, to ensure cohesion and negotiating power with other family firms. Such firms are small-scale, cutting Italy out of world-class global businesses, and have succession problems – it is hard to attract the best non-family talent in the first place, and the successor to an effective founder is likely to be less effective.

Decades of dependence on devaluation without financial discipline have led Italian firms by default into industries where competition on cost is critical: by definition, commodity industries such as textiles, steel and tiles. They are also the natural start-up industries for low-income countries hoping for economic emergence through export-led growth, for example Pacific Asia. Italy was thus in the first line of defence in the developed world – in effect, the 'weakest link'. Most major countries have seen a decline in their export market share, with that of the whole OECD decreasing some 10% in world trade share over ten years, reflecting (principally) the gains of China, whose share has increased 3½ times in ten years. But Italy's loss of 40% of its world trade share by volume in 12 years is by far the worst of the major world economies.

The flipside of undue focus on commodity industries is weakness in advanced ones such as high-tech and business services, including finance. Italian firms, perhaps unwittingly, took a huge gamble in 1999 by not taking out protection against Y2K (remember that?) and won handsomely on that bet. But the underlying reason, general neglect of high technology and its possibilities, has been a contributor to poor productivity performance. Thus, of major countries, Italian business spends about 1% of its value added on high-tech, compared with nearly twice that in Britain and France, 2½% in Germany, nearly 3% in the US and over 3% in Japan. Nor does Italy have a strong position in the high-value business service sectors to offset slow productivity growth in technology-led export industries where Japanese, German and other north European firms are strong.

How can Italy's costs be cut by 25%, relative to others (that is, from 133% of par to 100%)? Competitor countries are unlikely to help much. All the major exporters except China are in trouble, and deflation is possible in developed countries' CPIs, at least over the next few years. So the cut in costs needed is absolute rather than relative, with help unlikely from either others' inflation or productivity growth in Italy. To get Italian costs down by enough in cash terms to make them competitive is clearly an impossible task. And if wages were slashed, in a weak overall world economic environment, growth in Italy would be further hammered by falling domestic demand.

Ireland and Spain: seven fat years followed by seven lean years

Unlike Italy and Germany, Ireland and Spain gained major benefits from EMU membership for eight years. Their growth has been better than Britain's and far ahead of the dismal results achieved in the euro-zone core (Germany, France and Benelux), let alone Italy. EMU encourages such imbalances, exaggerating growth and inflation in Spain and Ireland, and curbing them in the core. It has widened financial imbalances dramatically. Fiscal policy has offset this – both countries were in budget surplus until the crisis struck – but only partially.

Ireland has managed remarkable multiple gains from EU membership. The EU was kind to it initially, as an agricultural and relatively poor nation. The Common Agricultural Policy and regional policies provided an abundance of cash. For the past 20 years it has benefited from extremely benign supply-side factors. People all over the world (many of Irish origin) have poured in capital, encouraged by low taxes, and have been anxious to work there. Land is plentiful, with a population lower than it was two centuries ago. Only a shortage of buildings constrained expansion – hence the huge, prolonged real estate price and building boom. This has been pumped up into a bubble by the euro umbrella, with interest rates suited more to the moribund core economies than the much smaller, dynamic fringes.

The upward distortion to growth in Spain and Ireland arising from EMU has led to major distortion of economic structure, chiefly a huge excess of real estate and construction activity. EMU specifically exaggerated their growth, as these sectors are particularly sensitive to credit. Shifts in interest rates have large effects on real estate asset values, with major knock-on effects on the incentive to build. As both countries ended the 1990s still needing a construction upswing to accommodate their growth in income and activity, EMU added fuel to an already vigorous boom.

What both Ireland and Spain needed at the peak of the boom in 2007 was:

- tight monetary policy – to curb real estate/construction excesses;
- fiscal surpluses – which were achieved, on a modest scale;
- devaluation, for different reasons in each case:
  - Spain is some 15–20% overvalued, not so completely beyond rescue as in Italy, but a severe inhibition to switching business lines from construction and real estate to other industries, when world markets are in any case depressed;
  - Ireland is not overvalued in historic cost terms like Spain, but its adjustment will involve, as in Britain, a simple reduction in income to reflect the shrunken prospective size of the key financial sector. The cut could most readily be achieved by devaluation in recognition of reduced buying power.

What they needed is one thing; what they got was the opposite, courtesy of the euro: a rising real effective exchange rate and even easier money. So, in the absence of key demand-management tools, these two countries have had to adjust by the only alternative: letting the boom rip until the supply side collapsed under its own weight. Now this has happened, Spain's cut in labour costs and Ireland's needed income cut are being or will be achieved by sharp deflation. After eight years of easy living, the crisis brought payback time, with Spain looking worse placed than Ireland.

Ireland's red-hot growth peaked at 8% on a ten-year moving

average basis in 2003, but remained close to 6% even as late as 2008, though GDP actually fell in that year. Spain's average shifted from 3% in the 1990s – only about 1% ahead of the euro-zone core – to nearly 4% in the past decade, 2% ahead. Both countries lost cost competitiveness as they outgrew their neighbours, sucking in capital and inducing current-account deficits, as imports soared and exports were relatively inhibited.

Irish financial balances never became as distorted as Spain's in the boom. Its current-account deficit only reached 5% of GDP in 2007, the private sector's deficit reaching 6%. The government took advantage of the prolonged boom to run a significant, though not huge, surplus over the years. The danger of unit labour cost overvaluation was somewhat offset by dynamic growth of productivity, helping exports as well as restraining costs, so that the current deficit remained within bounds even though growth was torrid. Being strongly integrated in international finance, Ireland was hit by the subprime crisis earlier than Spain.

Spain's expansion was much more exclusively focused on real estate and construction than Ireland's. One result was that growth of productivity, only marginally positive in the ten years up to the crisis, was held back by the lack of development in high-value industries. Rapid wage growth fed straight into unit labour costs, cutting competitiveness and ensuring the boom caused fast growth in the current deficit. It may be that the type of construction was a factor. People were going to Ireland to work, to Spain for holidays and retirement homes. This could have affected the degree of builders' cost discipline. Almost certainly, the more stratified Spanish labour market – depending on either unionised, inflexible labour or low-wage, low-skilled, often immigrant labour – inhibited productivity growth. The focus on extensive growth, with major gains in employment, rather than intensive growth of output per worker, contributed to the dependence on external financing, with the current deficit peaking at 10% of GDP in 2007. For both countries, dramatic 2009 GDP falls have sharply worsened budget balances and cut imports.

Spain's construction boom was more extravagant than Ireland's. Starting from a little over 8% of GDP at the peak of the last boom in 2000, Spanish construction raised its share of GDP by four percentage points over the seven years to 2007. Ireland's went up by little over two points in the same period. Their respective shares of 12% and 10% in 2007 compares with 4½% in the US, down from its 5% 2006 peak. Yet the US had a housing boom too. To make the comparison less biased by the low level of US construction costs – Germany's construction share, for example, only fell below America's in 2001 despite its prolonged slump after 1994 – we can include real estate services, where the excessive level of US rewards was instrumental in keeping the boom going well after its economic basis was undermined. Here too Ireland compares well with Spain, as its real estate service sector was responsible for 8% of GDP in both 2000 and 2007. Spain's went up from 8% to nearly 12%, while the US share for this sector, already over 12% in 2000, remained at that level until 2007.

In the last couple of years of the debt bubble both Ireland and Spain became less competitive by about 10% of additional relative unit labour cost. But here again – and perhaps because of the divergent tendencies of business productivity – Ireland looks better than Spain. Spain has seen its relative unit labour costs move up by one-third in the past decade. Without doubt, it was undervalued on entry into the euro in 1999, so it is probably some

15–20% overvalued now. By contrast, Ireland went into the euro way below its previous relative unit labour cost level, and did not suffer too serious a rise in relative costs in the strong-euro period from early 2002. It is hard to regard the current level of costs as serious overvaluation.

But Ireland, like Britain, has been overweight in finance, which is likely to be a weak industry in the medium term. Just as Britain has had a major drop in sterling to accommodate the genuine loss of relative income implied by shrinkage of financial services, so should Ireland. This implies overvaluation, therefore, but probably less than Spain's (and far less crippling than Italy's).

Ireland's other major advantage over Spain is high per-person income. By the time of the crisis, Irish per-person GDP was 25–30% higher than that of the UK, Germany and France, and though this comes down to about a 10% premium at the level of GNP, it is still a healthy margin to be playing with in a belt-tightening phase. Ireland's recession was about 3–4% worse than that of the three European majors on a full-year basis in both 2008 and 2009, with the same relative slippage likely in 2010. But such results would still leave the country with about the same GNP, and a 15% premium in GDP, per person. Furthermore, assuming continued national solvency, Ireland could grow from 2011 onwards with its flexible, service-based economy and better-sustained industrial activity. Effectively, the crisis could require Ireland to give up for the time being its income advantage over the European Big 3 (Germany, the UK and France), but with a good chance of resuming growth at least as fast as them from 2011 onwards.

In Spain, the income problem is acute. To be sure, the country overtook Italy by 5% in per-person GDP (though it would be as true to say that Italy has managed to fall behind it), and its recessionary drop in GDP is quite close to the European average. But there are grounds for doubt about Spanish GDP data in this recession – unemployment is up by 12 percentage points to 20% of the labour force – and strong grounds for thinking it has poor recovery potential in future years. Chiefly, this is a question of serious overvaluation on the cost side and the effects of ten years' zero productivity growth on the product side.

Ireland and Spain were both strongly on the deficit-country side of global imbalances, but whereas Spain was the more extravagant in terms of current-account deficit, on the banking side Ireland took the prize – within EMU, that is. Irish banks' risk assets were twice the share of GDP in France and Germany. The only good news is that Irish banks (having had plenty to keep themselves busy with at home) did not go down the German road (largely avoided too by the French) of buying dubious mortgage-related CDOs and other assets marketed by US investment banks.

Spanish adjustment will not lead to serious growth until costs have been hammered, global recovery has been (unexpectedly) brisk, or Spain has left the euro. Even the first of these three looks remote, as in the year to the third quarter of 2009 the hourly wage index increased by over 4%, despite the recession, though cuts in hours meant the weekly/monthly gain was 1% less. What happened was that temporary contract workers, often immigrants, had been taken on under contract in the boom, and at lower wages than the permanent, job-protected Spanish labour force operating under older laws. The temps got laid off first, so average labour costs went up despite recession and soaring unemployment Of course when wage adjustment does come, Spain, in the absence of strong recovery elsewhere, will be held back from fast growth by the weakness of domestic consumption.

Irish wage adjustment has got somewhat further. The Irish economy is entering a period of profound deflation, as its need for devaluation cannot be satisfied by leaving the euro, yet cannot be avoided in a small flexible economy. The CPI in March 2010 was down 3% from a year earlier, contrasting with increases of 1.4% in Spain and 1.4% in the euro zone as a whole. In Britain, where the adjustment needed is similar in kind to Ireland's, the CPI was up 3.4%, reflecting the achievement of lower relative costs by devaluation and the consequent upward effect of more costly imports.

This rapid Irish price adjustment process is further evidence that its economy has the capacity to generate renewed growth (from a lower level) within the foreseeable future. This cannot be said of Spain. In the eight quarters since recession started, real Irish GDP fell 13½%, but nominal GDP fell 17½%. Being in EMU entails exactly this kind of willingness to adjust nominal incomes downwards. So far none of the major countries in the euro have shown this, not even Germany. Ireland will probably have to live with falling prices for at least a year more, by when our forecast is that general deflation will have taken over in both the US and the euro zone as a whole. So rising prices are not on the horizon for the medium term. This seemingly not too gloomy forecast for Ireland looks nastier when it is remembered that the debts in the economy are all in nominal euros, increasing the real burden on current incomes with every cent of their decline. The economy may resume growth, but real spendable income will lag behind.

Spain, like Italy with a population anaesthetised from any free-market pain, is clearly incapable of coping with the challenge of sustaining a cost-competitive and flexible supply side in a world that – ultimately – takes no prisoners. Where wages are advancing by 3–4%, they need to be falling by the same amount. Yet this will never be advocated in the current economic situation as the countries that are competitive – in Europe, Germany and its immediate surrounds – refuse to spend their income. So downward wage adjustment in Mediterranean Europe would simply add to the continent-wide misery, as spending would spiral down with income.

In the Grimm Brothers' tale, Hänsel and Gretel outwit the wicked witch and escape the oven, in the process rescuing their predecessors who had succumbed. But with Ireland and Spain as Hänsel and Gretel (whichever is which) such a happy outcome is unlikely. Ireland may escape with a sharply painful flash frying, but Spain looks to be in the oven roasting at medium-high temperature for a long time.

Greek pips squeak as government deficits soar

The key financial variables of Greece reflect the fact that the country shares Spain's huge deficit problem, but also Ireland's lack of serious overvaluation. The implications of the financial data are that Italy and Greece should not have been allowed into EMU to start with, and have done little or nothing to accept the implicit discipline of membership. Greece, unlike Italy, has at least benefited from membership in that growth accelerated – doubled in fact. By contrast, Italian growth has been slower since it joined EMU than it was before, and the single currency structure is partly responsible. Greek inflation has been about 1½% a year higher than that of Germany and France, twice the premium of Italy's.

While exchange rate and competitiveness fundamentals argue

that Italy and Spain are worse placed than Greece, the financial ratios are worse in Greece. The current-account deficit to
be financed has been remarkable at over 14% of GDP in 2007
and 2008, followed by 11% in 2009. Initially, this reflected a
private-sector deficit. But the government deficit has mounted in
the crisis, reaching 13% of GDP in 2009, and comes on top of
net government debt of 86% of GDP at the end of 2009, plus, no
doubt, potential assumption of all or part of the private sector's
recently run-up of debts if the economy remains stagnant or in
recession, as is likely.

For the eight months from March 2009's global financial nadir
until early November, the rising tide of investor enthusiasm for
risk assets 'lifted all ships'. But then the atmosphere soured. The
headlines started with a good story: high-flying Dubai crashes.
Behind them lies the more important story: Chinese tightening,
because of severe overheating and rapidly rising inflation (see
Chapter 5). The positive aspect of Chinese tightening is that the
end of the recovery phase for risk-asset prices checked the euro's
ascent: Mediterranean Europe needs every bit of competitive help
it can get. The bad news is that continued Chinese export market-
share gains combined with moves to restrict its domestic demand
are a pincer movement on the European economy, in conjunction
with US import substitution. The ugly news is the flipside of the
good news: renewed bearishness in many risk-asset prices – a
category that has Greek bonds front and centre.

Even after the IMF-led patch-up of Greek finances, and the
start of a savage austerity programme, ten-year Greek bonds
still yield 4–5% more than their German equivalents. With net
debt approaching 100% of GDP, and the latter falling as deflation bites, the impact of such high rates brings Greece close to

a tipping point where some form of default is unavoidable. The problem is that after the global crash and partial recovery, the world has started to discriminate much more than in the blind, correlated days of crisis, panic and rebound. With China potentially no longer such a large source of domestic demand locomotion to the rest of the world, and Germany only likely to fill that gap on a minimal scale, if at all, growth will depend on continued government borrowing, rather than a major reduction of the Eurasian savings glut. The focus on government debt as the weak point of the global financial system is likely to sharpen.

Just as with banks, large countries, unlike small ones, may be too big to fail. The US and British position is discussed in Chapter 9. But Keynesian arguments for a fiscal stimulus to offset recession and unemployment are ineffective if investor confidence requires tightening the budget in small countries with proportionately large deficits, especially those with large outstanding debt already. Greece looks closest to Ireland, but without Ireland's excellent starting point of no net government debt at the end of 2007. The Greek economy is likely to remain in prolonged recession, driven by severe tightening of government policy. The structural or policy budget deficit is scheduled to go down five percentage points in 2010 from 10.4% of GDP in 2009 (up from 7.5% in 2008). As a result, with the cyclical effects of the recession adding to the deficit, the cut in the actual outcome is scheduled to be four percentage points. (Compare the cut from 6% of GDP to 3% in Italy's budget deficit over two years between 1996 and 1998, to qualify for EMU membership – thought ferocious at the time.)

Clearly, for Greece to reduce deficits further in a slow-growth world, policy will mean savage deflation, implying rising unemployment and negative feedback in the deficit-reduction process from the cyclical harm to the balance of tax revenue and social spending. The scale of what is being attempted, and the socio-political damage the programme will cause in Greece, mean that the deficit-reduction targets may well not be met. Meanwhile, German public anger at being asked to bail out self-indulgent Greeks has pushed Germany to the point of exacting conditions for any bail-out that weaken sharply any sense of EMU community spirit. But the purpose of the exercise, of course, is to enable Greek deficits to be financed. The divisions revealed by the crisis make the logical development of EMU – fusion into a proto-nation state – less probable. But the current halfway house is almost certainly untenable, and the alternative is for EMU to dissolve, or shrink to its core: Germany, Benelux, France and Austria. Investors could easily get the perception from the recent wrangling that Greece at least, and probably others, cannot hold onto EMU membership. In that case its borrowing terms would worsen further, and with them the budgetary position, in a vicious circle. So the political processes to make Greek deficits and debt financeable may have made them unfinanceable anyhow.

A collapse of confidence in Greek credit will spread to Spain, Portugal and Italy, with the threat (or release) of Greece seceding from the monetary union. This would render their national credit almost impossible to sustain, not to mention their economic growth, and probably force most of them to follow Greece out of the euro. In all probability the long-term prospects of all these countries would be much improved by abandoning the inappropriate yoke of EMU membership. But ten years of complacent delusions as to the stabilising benefits of the – in reality profoundly destabilising – euro mean their situations have now deteriorated to the point that the future is likely to be extremely painful whether they stay in or drop out.

European export gluttons to suck wind

Germany and its surrounding countries in north-central Europe – Benelux, the Nordic countries, Switzerland and Austria – have fallen into a trap through their cautious approach to economic policy and their determination to build up overseas assets against the future retirement of the baby-boomers. Their private saving surplus over private investment – partly spurred by corporate restructuring as well as demographic effects – reached about 8% of GDP by 2007, up 2½ percentage points from 2003, the start of recovery. Meanwhile, over the same four years, aggressive fiscal tightening led to the group being in budget surplus by 2007, a shift of about 3–4 percentage points of GDP. These combined to raise what had been modest current-account surpluses by close to 6% of GDP, to reach 2007's 8%, $520 billion. So how did this lurch into export dependency leave them more vulnerable to the crisis arising from the credit crunch – ironically, more vulnerable than the deficit countries (except those unwise enough to be in EMU)?

EMU's north Mediterranean problem children (Club Med) constitute one-third of EMU's GDP. North-Central Europe (NCE), for which the proxy here will be Germany, is larger than Club Med by two-thirds, including its non-EMU economies, the Nordic countries (mostly in the EU but not EMU) and Switzerland (in neither). The NCE economies heavily depend on exports to one another and to the rest of Europe, which is in turn having its income sapped by the link to NCE in the euro. NCE exporters

Figure 24   **North-central Europe: current-account balances**
        % GDP

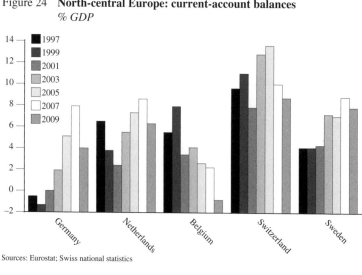

Sources: Eurostat; Swiss national statistics

are too competitive exactly because Club Med is uncompetitive, and this stops the latter growing. Locked together, neither group can advance without some help from the rest of the world – or determined and permanent offsetting of excessive NCE private savings with structural government deficits.

The rest of the world is unlikely to be helpful. Continental Europe's largest export market is Britain, which has had its own severe recession and has improved its relative competitiveness with a major devaluation of about one-quarter vis-à-vis the euro. While the British recovery in 2010 could be quite brisk, import substitution and export gains could reduce the benefit to continental Europe. Similar currency-related factors apply to the US recovery, which in any case has probably peaked, to be followed by more moderate growth for a year or two. Nor will China be much help, as explained in Chapter 5.

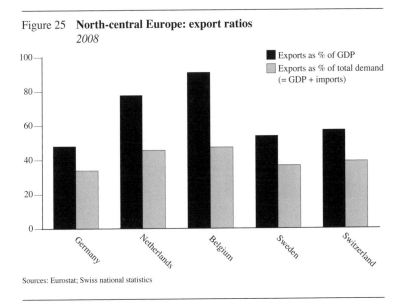

Figure 25 **North-central Europe: export ratios**
2008

Legend:
- Exports as % of GDP
- Exports as % of total demand (= GDP + imports)

Sources: Eurostat; Swiss national statistics

The NCE economies clustered round Germany almost exactly equal Germany in aggregate GDP and current-account surplus. The German numbers multiplied by two roughly describe the story for NCE. Though NCE's structural surplus at full employment (2007) was $520 billion, it was only about two-thirds of that in 2009, owing to export-led recession. In effect, these economies have been taking a free ride, generating income and building up assets by selling into the domestic demand of the deficit economies, fuelled by borrowing that should not have taken place.

Figure 25 shows the importance of exports to these countries. In Germany, the 47% of GDP current-price export ratio becomes 52% at the constant-price measure used for GDP growth. (Exports have fallen in price relative to the rest of GDP.) A better measure, which excludes the effect of the huge import-export through-put of the entrepôt economies in this group, is to compare exports

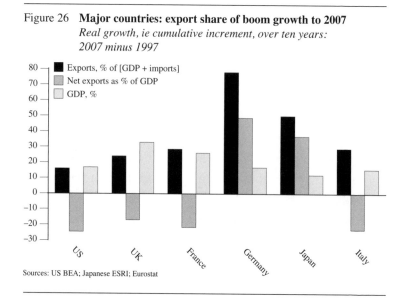

Figure 26 **Major countries: export share of boom growth to 2007**
Real growth, ie cumulative increment, over ten years: 2007 minus 1997

Exports, % of [GDP + imports]
Net exports as % of GDP
GDP, %

US   UK   France   Germany   Japan   Italy

Sources: US BEA; Japanese ESRI; Eurostat

with GDP plus imports, which defines total supply (and demand) in the economy. On this basis, exports vary between one-third of total supply and demand for German and nearly half for Belgium.

Figure 26 shows how much major countries have grown and how much they have depended on exports. The dismal growth performance of Germany and Italy (and Japan) is a second reason for exports taking such a large share of their growth. The total-demand/total-supply concept is most useful and relevant here, that is, GDP plus imports. This is the best measure of total through-put in the economy. So the growth of real exports between 1997 and 2007 is shown as a percentage of the real growth of GDP plus imports. This enlarged measure of the economy takes account of the differing trade shares in different economies and the shift towards openness, larger trade shares, over time. The ten years in question were good ones, with two booms (1998–2000 and

2004–07) and only one mild recession (2001–02), so the weakness of German and Italian growth is particularly evident. It is a peculiar point that Germany's far greater cost and product competitiveness, and financial strength, nonetheless yielded about the same ten-year growth as Italy, and that its greater concentration on exports and surpluses meant actual real consumer welfare grew less than Italy's.

Now that domestic demand has collapsed globally, it is little surprise that it has hit hardest in the countries with structurally deficient domestic demand to start with – those with a savings glut. The mechanism of this collapse was the trade crash. Thus NCE's recession in 2009 was about the same as Britain's, with Germany's being worse – and nearly twice as bad as that of the other debt-laden 'sinner', the US. As deficit countries gradually correct their deficits and excessive private-sector debts, NCE will be unlikely to see a revival of its exports to generate growth in the style of 2005–07, especially as the Chinese juggernaut increasingly erodes their world market share. Only with a structural shift to domestic spending can growth become adequate.

Germany's excess saving problem is in the household sector. The post-second-world-war baby boom did not get fully under way until the 1950s, so the bulge generation is currently in its late-career, maximum-saving time of life. The household savings surplus over housing investment was 5½% of GDP in 2007, since when fear induced by the recession has raised it further. Business-sector vigilance over wasting money, and lowered costs after years of restrained wage growth, meant that business cash flow exceeded capital outlays by 2% of GDP in 2007. Export-led recession should have sent business into deficit by 2009, but government employment subsidies and the slashing of capital spending and inventory have made up some of the potential net cash flow loss. The government balance was ½% of GDP in 2007, so that the combined financial surpluses of these three domestic sectors totalled 8% of GDP, and that was 2007's current-account surplus. The current surplus fell to 5% of GDP in 2009 as exports led the economy down. The government deficit of more than 3%, mostly reflecting recession rather than stimulative policy, offset the remainder of the private surplus.

Retirement of the baby-boomers, after which their savings may be minimal, should start over the next five years. Those born in 1950 will reach 65 in 2015; for those born in 1964 the corresponding date is 2029. From 2015 or so, a slow but steady subsidence of the household financial surplus can be expected from these natural, demographic causes. But in the near term, the economy can expect little stimulus from this quarter. In the absence of adequate medium-term stimulus from exports, once the current inventory snap-back has faded, the only way the economy can grow is by raising its consumption through deliberate deficit budgeting by the government.

The German government has covertly, though only temporarily, dismantled its insistence on budget balancing as the priority of fiscal policy. It took a temporary step in the car market: an incentive programme to encourage trade-ins of gas-guzzling old bangers for fuel-efficient new cars had a strong response. This helped sustain consumption in early 2009. But of course the cars being replaced were old ones, soon likely to be replaced anyhow, so that the downside of this measure is falling sales at the end of 2009 and in 2010 – not just to where they might have been anyhow, but lower, to reflect the replacement sales brought forward.

Figure 27 **German export volume and manufacturing output**
Jan-08 = 100

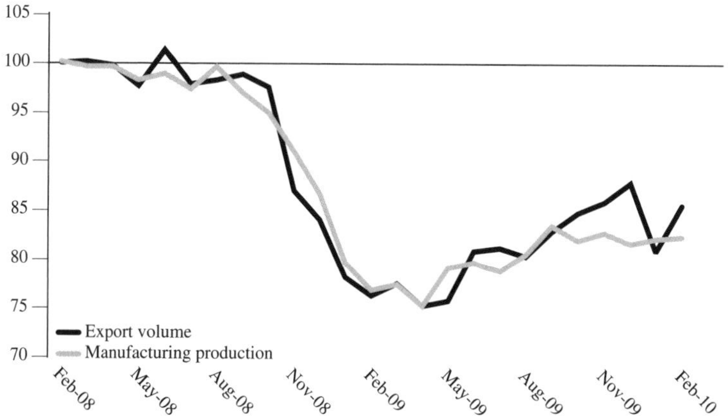

Source: Bundesbank

A crucial policy in sustaining consumer spending has been financial support for firms to continue employing workers who would otherwise have been laid off, by paying a portion of their wages. This has limited unemployment to a little over 8%, below 2007 levels and little above those in 2008. But the 3.4 million unemployed were supplemented by 1.5 million short-time workers at the April 2009 peak (down to 0.9 million by March 2010). So unemployed plus short-time peaked at about 12% and is now just under 10% of the labour force. The support scheme for short-time work is currently extended to late 2010.

The relapse in car sales since spring 2009 contributed to the rapid fall in real consumer spending in the second half of 2009 and early 2010. Now the tax cuts agreed between the Christian Democrats and the Free Democrats as part of the coalition deal last autumn have been revoked by Chancellor Angela Merkel in response to the Greek crisis bail-out package – to which they are, of course, completely irrelevant. This extremely damaging decision, combined with likely further hikes in saving by nervous German consumers contemplating the further degradation of their currency by EMU, means that after a brief boost from lesser inventory liquidation in mid-2010, the German economy could be adding to the virtual certainty of renewed recession in continental Europe, with a significant danger of depression. It completes a decade of disastrous German economic policy blunders.

A major danger is that firms, confronted with clear evidence of continuing inadequate demand, move to downsize capacity. Exports have recovered by only half from their 25% crash in the six months to spring 2009. The core manufacturing sector has lost over 15% of its sales. The revival of domestic demand in Germany was to have been helped by the 1½% of GDP structural increase in 2010's budget deficit, that is, policy-related rather than recession-driven. But that is effectively undone by the revocation of planned tax cuts. Meanwhile, weak disposable income growth and higher saving could continue. So far German business confidence in the recovery has continued to mount, and (unlike America) Germany has the bulk of the inventory snap-back in 2010 as liquidation was a huge 2½% of GDP in late 2009. But the flat-lining of industrial production cannot be ignored forever by businesses whose unit costs have been boosted. The rising savings rate, motivated by fear, could be self-fulfilling if substantial cuts in capacity are implemented. As 2010 draws on and the Club Med recession intensifies, recovery is likely to stall.

The German government and its apologists overstate their case in their belief in principle, first, in a balanced budget, presented as a belief not a rational argument, and second, in Ricardian

Figure 28 **German household net saving and government deficit**
%

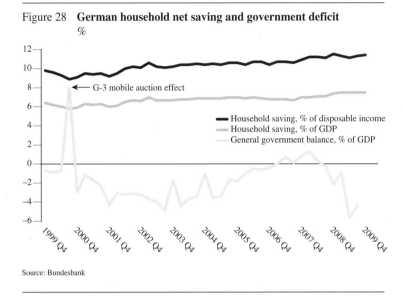

← G-3 mobile auction effect

Household saving, % of disposable income
Household saving, % of GDP
General government balance, % of GDP

Source: Bundesbank

equivalence. The latter argues roughly as follows: households believe that any tax cuts they receive involving a government deficit will be clawed back in future, so they save them. Quite apart from the massive and highly implausible assumption that households are far-sighted, this theory is impossible to square with the evidence. As Figure 28 shows, the savings rate has been steady over time with a mild ten-year upward drift. Yet earlier in the last decade the budget deficit was 4% of GDP, while 2007 saw a surplus. Under Ricardian equivalence this positive shift of the budget should have released Germans from the fear of future imposts and led to a cut in the savings rate that – on this theory – was earlier boosted by that fear. Yet no such thing happened. The savings rate carried on gently up. Nor has the recent lurch into deficit halted the upward drift. So we can safely assume that if the German government wished to run a deficit, to stimulate domestic demand with tax cuts, for example, Germans would enjoy the extra income and spend it, like people everywhere else. The strong response to the 2009 car incentive programme supports this view.

So the problem lies squarely with Germany's ideological belief in budget balancing. The previous grand coalition government even passed a constitutional amendment (effectively now beyond repeal) requiring deficits never to be more than ½% of GDP from 2012. But there is no empirical, utilitarian rationale for this. It appears to be an item of faith rather than thought. The implied comparison of the *öffentliche haushalt* (public household, or public sector) with a virtuous Swabian housewife is meaningless. Why not aim for a 2% surplus – or a 2% deficit? Or 4% (either way)? What is the magic in that zero? In the real world, a country that has consistent private-sector financial deficits might well be advised to aim for consistent budget surplus – unless the private sector offers huge profit opportunities that are readily open to overseas capital. Likewise, a country like Germany that has a large private-sector surplus already has enough, probably too much, 'Swabian housewifery' and should offset this tendency with a public-sector deficit, if only to avoid becoming too dependent on exports.

Germany dealt well with the distortions that inevitably arose from unification in 1990. The current behaviour pattern and policy was set in 2002, when the country effectively refused to participate in the global recovery from the recession following the stockmarket bubble and bust. If we measure growth from the end of the European recession, the end of 2001, Figure 29 shows how appalling German economic performance has been. By the end of 2009, eight years later, after a slight recovery, German

Figure 29 **Real GDP since end of last recession: G-6 economies**
2001Q4 = 100

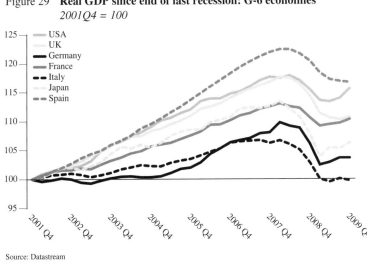

Source: Datastream

cumulative growth was 3½%, less than ½% a year, compared with nearly 11% in Britain and over 10% in France, both of them unimpressive at less than 1½% a year. The US and Spain were also below par, but up about 16%, or 2% a year. Germany was bracketed between the sick man of the world, Japan (up 6% over eight years) and the sick man of Europe, Italy (slightly down).

Everybody that looked at the real Italy, rather than the fantasy of how it might become part of some federal European economy rather like the US, knew that it would be crushed by EMU membership. But Germany has done little better. Germans complain about subsidising Greeks, but they should really direct their ire at Italians. Whereas the eight-year growth of real GDP was 3½% in Germany and slightly down in Italy, the eight-year growth of real consumption was the reverse: ½% in Germany and 3½% in Italy. Yet without those Italians spending away, German output, jobs, incomes and consumption would have been even worse. The folly of the miser indeed.

This path to nowhere was initiated by savage and unnecessary budgetary rigour, starting in 2002 under the former finance minister, Hans Eichel. The economy did not grow at all in more than three years from late 2001 to early 2005. It then rose some 10% over three years, but only because of deficit-country delinquency. The US house-price peak of late 2005–early 2006 should have led to progressive cuts in US borrowing – certainly in the opinion of German officialdom. If that had happened, German growth over the past eight years would have been even feebler than it was, as the chief growth patch would not have occurred.

It is common to hear Germany's poor economic performance justified by referring to weak demographics. But this is a fallacy. It is true that in the run-up to the crisis, Germany's working-age population was falling at about ½% a year. But the participation of working-age people in the labour force outweighed this decline in the age group so that in fact the labour force rose by ½% a year. So shortage of labour input was no excuse for poor growth. The reality is that output per worker-hour has been steadily falling, from annual averages of around 2% a year in the 1990s to a mere ½% a year in the latest economic cycle (using a 7½-year average to reflect the cycle from the end of recession in late 2001 to the low point in spring 2009). Slow growth reflects steadily declining German competitiveness, the opposite of what its apologists loudly proclaim. The German economy is only competitive in the cost sense, because its labour has been repressed and is yoked to Club Med and France, where productivity gains have been even worse and wages are still growing.

The easiest way to see how poorly Germany has done is to

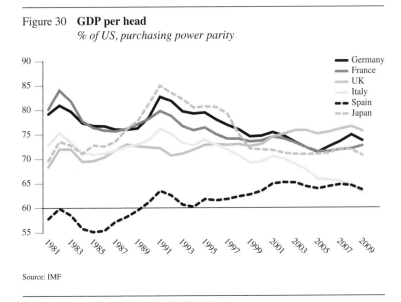

Figure 30 **GDP per head**
% of US, purchasing power parity

Source: IMF

look at GDP per person adjusted for different price levels in different countries – the so-called purchasing-power parity (PPP). In Figure 29 this measure of income per head is shown as a percentage of that of the US. On this basis, Germany reached 80% of US income levels in the early 1980s as a result of the long postwar boom and catch-up. Since then it has fallen steadily back to the 72–75% region. French performance has been equally feeble, and Italy has been worse as it has gone down further from a less good post-second-world-war peak. Spain has done well, catching up with Italy, but is now threatened with a long decline, owing to the poverty of its policy options within the euro. Britain has improved from its dismal ratio in the 1970s, worse than France and Germany today, to a little above them, around 75–76%. Basically, any failure to catch up, or at least remain stable, vis-à-vis the US from these 70–80% levels means a country is doing badly.

A purely solipsistic defence of German policy might be that the country needs net saving through current-account surpluses to provide for future years, when retirement of the baby-boomers will shrink the working-age population and potential economic growth, so that income from foreign assets can make up the difference. But this point only holds if the rest of the world is a willing recipient of German capital, so it yields a decent return. In current conditions, this is wishful thinking. German excess saving is contributing to conditions that will at best ensure both falling income – from reduced terms of trade – and negligible to negative real total return on capital. The solipsism arises from the fact that the same logic of providing for baby-boomers' retirement would indicate net current-account surpluses for the US and Canada, all of Europe and Japan. In that case, the extremely damaging savings glut we have had would be remembered as a mere flea bite by comparison, and the world would crash into deep depression – of which there is, of course, a significant chance anyhow, given that global private-sector excess saving has already become huge.

The problem for Germany in depending on huge net exports to offset a domestic savings glut is that the reception of its salespeople is bound to get tougher in the new, supposedly deleveraging, probably modest, Anglo-Saxon growth period – always assuming we are right to forecast a recovery at all. In an extreme scenario – not applicable to Britain, being in the EU – the concentration of new borrower-country debt in the government (rather than, in the past, households) might incline US policymakers to say: 'Why should we run up national debts for our children to pay off, just to generate jobs and income in Shanghai and Stuttgart. Let's slap on an import surcharge to reduce the budget deficit and bias the job creation and income to our own taxpayers.' This kind of attack on free trade would be the logical consequence of large, persistent savings gluts. Free trade is a utilitarian principle, not an absolute value, so such an argument is hard to refute.

While Germany, China, Japan and the other savings-glut countries are certainly taking major risks with the structure of free trade built up over the past 60 years, we may well be able to get through this crisis without such an extreme breakdown. But growth in the US and the UK, while it should remain positive, is likely to be weaker over the medium term than recently – which in the US case was already a poor cycle by past standards. In that case, savings-glut countries will probably have to accept much worse terms of trade development – that is, less real income gain from physical net export gains – than in the past.

But Germany's terms of trade have become poorer even in the favourable conditions of the 1990s and 2000s to date. It is little surprise that a country that has depended on exports for nearly 80% of its total gain in real GDP plus imports – in effect, leaving its citizens with no growth in real spendable income – has had to price itself into its overseas markets. Over the past 20 years, Figure 31 shows there has been a major contrast between Germany's 7–8% fall in terms of trade – in effect subtracting 0.4% a year in real income terms from the already feeble GDP growth trend of about 1¼–1½% – and the British improvement of 5% or so, adding real income to its 2½% GDP growth trend.

During the recent globalisation period, when Pacific Asian countries led by China have been pricing themselves into world markets on a massive scale, the British experience of reduced world trade share but in higher value-added business is what would be expected of an advanced economy. Germany had to,

Figure 31   **Export/import prices, goods and services**
              1988 Q4 = 100

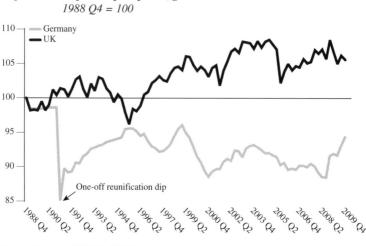

Sources: Bundesbank; UK National Statistics

in effect, discount its high-end goods to win sufficient markets, so it has been a poor performer over the past 20 years. In the much-reduced context of the next several years, the reduction in its terms of trade could be more painful, though perhaps partly offset by falling commodity prices.

Once net exports have been achieved, at whatever cost in terms of trade, savings-glut countries may find the returns available on investing their surpluses are negative. As with the terms of trade, any worsening on this score would be from an already unsatisfactory base. Net asset holdings have been subject to massive capital losses recently that may only partly show up in the net investment income account. But in 2008, a current-account surplus of $245 billion showed up as less than a $50 billion gain in net foreign assets, which had fallen in 2007. Germans in effect work hard to produce goods that increasingly have to be discounted, and then have to watch that weaker flow of income slashed by poor invest-ment returns. German economic policy is a solipsistic denial of reality. The world of the next five years could have less need for financial investors, owing to recent excesses, other than those keen to finance government deficits. The return on assets pain-fully built up at the cost of worse German terms of trade could prove even poorer than the negative returns of the recent past.

8

Japan: sliding downhill too fast to catch?

Japan's late 1980s bubble was followed by its long night of the 1990s. This gives some useful hints about the forces at work globally today – by no coincidence, Japan has been a major part of the current Eurasian surplus problem. There are huge differences between Japan's particular experience and the global story in recent years. But there are also points in common, and lessons that can be learned by policymakers, if they so wish, and by the rest of us, if we wish to understand what is going on and what the future may hold. A crucial common point is that a structural excess of savings has been a major part of Japan's problems for the better part of 20 years (much longer, some would argue).

For more than ten years Japan has had persistent, large government deficits resulting in government debt that is 100% of GDP, net of financial assets, and 200% of GDP gross. Yet it has also had persistent deflation. This gives the lie to commentators who assume that current large advanced country deficits will necessarily cause a lurch into inflation – though the Japanese might wish that it would. If the US Fed could create inflation by printing money, perhaps it would. The real danger, however, is not that it will, but that it can't – that the world is now, at least in part, a globalised Japan.

Until the mid-1980s, Japan had a high personal (household) saving rate, but a conventional rate of business saving (that is, depreciation plus retained profit). In the US, for example, business savings have for the past 25 years been in the region of 12–13% of GDP. In Japan they were just above this in the 1980s, but for a country then with a trend growth rate of nearly 5% – still in catch-up mode rather than a mature economy – it was not out of line. As the late 1980s bubble developed, business saving pushed upwards to around 17–18%. Household saving remained high. The boom boosted government tax receipts and its accounts went into surplus. The combination of private saving and government balance moved to 28% of GDP, up by 5–6 percentage points over 5–6 years.

This was excessive saving at the national level. Because the bubble involved – in fact was led by – strong business investment, industrial capacity soared. Excess capacity held down inflation. Monetary policy, seeing little inflation, was not particularly tight. So the current-account surplus was not particularly large: the savings were being used in the home market for overinvestment. This behaviour and policy mix (but not the current-account position) provided a fairly clean analogy with the US bubble of 1998–2000 that was the first-round effect ten years later of excessive Eurasian savings, especially in the Asian Tiger countries after the Asian crisis.

After the similarities in generation of the two bubbles – each reflecting huge liquidity expressing itself in asset prices rather than consumer price inflation – there was further similarity in the leveraging up of business with debt. But Japan's bubble was a lot more noxious than the 1998–2000 US bubble for a number of reasons:

- As well as a stockmarket bubble, real estate reached ridiculous prices. (This was the period when the Emperor's Palace garden became of higher value than the state of California.) In the long 1990–2003 bear market, real estate as well as stock prices fell a cumulative 80% or so.
- Japan's demographic trends were changing. From labour force growth in the 1980s, it slowed to stagnation and then a falling working-age population in the 1990s. This tended to increase saving (late-career) and simultaneously lower capital spending needs, especially on construction. So the excess of saving over investment (that is, the demand deficiency) was aggravated.
- The late 1980s marked the end of Japan's fast-growth catch-up development. The growth trend in the 1980s was just under 5%, well ahead of the US and western Europe. In the 1990s, only partly through the effects of the working-age population reversal, the GDP growth trend fell dramatically to about 1%.
- The sharp fall in trend growth meant that the old habit of loading firms with debt would not be justified by growing out of trouble. Debt ratios in Japan were higher in 1990 than the peaks in the US ten years later.
- US policy took a year or two to react fully to the bubble bursting and firms were restructuring hard by the end of 2001. But Japan was in denial from 1990 until 1996, during which time debt ratios and excess capacity got much worse.
- The Japanese top-down, directed development system had worked well in securing catch-up growth, but proved a serious liability once economic maturity was achieved. The shift to a bottom-up, market-based system with firms aiming for shareholder value is incomplete and has been a big wrench.

Between 1990 and 1997, the year Japan finally took on the full challenge of its bubble, government debt rose from 60% to 100% of GDP, and the lurch into major deficit had become chronic dependency. The reason for Japan's delay was that its bubble posed a far deeper challenge to Japanese society, politics and policymaking than the US bubble. Japan in 1990 was a consensus-driven, top-down, collectivist society, economy and polity. My Lombard Street Research colleague, Brian Reading, called it 'not capitalism with warts, but communism with beauty spots'. Business pursued sales, not profits. Workers enjoyed the lifetime employment system, in which they were tied to employers, and benefited from company pensions, health and social security, mortgages and housing, and of course salaries and bonuses. The corrupt nexus of the Liberal Democratic Party (LDP), the bureaucracy and locally based real estate interests, bound together by the tradition of cabinet-level unanimity policed by the civil service, sorted out the spoils at both the national and local level. Business looked to Japan Inc for the direction of policy.

When the bubble burst, the various Japanese parties thought it was simply a particularly nasty cyclical experience. Businesses did not realise that future gains in output and incomes would require decision-making reoriented to profit maximisation and shareholder value, if the legacy of gross excess capacity and debt were to be worked off. This point was strengthened by the end of easy catch-up and the need for market forces and price signals to drive decisions once the economy is operating near the technological frontier. Initially, Japanese companies cut capital spending sharply and simply waited for growth to revive. But the excess saving was structural. While business capital expenditure was cut to 15% of GDP – still at that level well above the corresponding

US ratio, despite the latter's faster growth – and housing fell sharply owing to population slowdown, the private savings rate edged upwards from 26% to 29% of GDP. This ensured a chronic deficiency of demand.

The adjustment route chosen was a continuation of previous habits, without the change of behaviour that was needed. A surge of government investment projects provided the 'iron triangle' of LDP politicians, bureaucrats and local business people with huge spoils to share. And the spending was needed – a Keynesian deficit boost to demand to avoid what would probably otherwise have been a slump or depression. By 1995, interest rates had been lowered close to zero (there to remain) as the yen spiked to the low 80s against the dollar. But the government's shift into a deficit of 5% of GDP was also crucial to sustaining demand. As the yen fell, some growth revived into early 1997. For a while, Japanese businesses may have thought the worst was over.

At that point the government decided to claw back towards budget balance with tax increases. This was much criticised at the time, but looks better in retrospect. As it turned out, the Asian crisis that started several months later affected Japan as well, but what was less appreciated was that even with only modest growth the economy was 3% overheated in spring 1997. The sustainable trend growth rate had fallen so far that only mild growth by past standards took the economy over the speed limit. The time for addressing the true societal, political and supply-side issues had arrived.

Sadly, in the six or seven wasted years, as well as the much higher government debt burden, Japan's businesses had raised their debt from rather under six times gross operating cash flow (depreciation plus pre-interest profit) to just under seven times. The mountain to be climbed was higher and steeper. The makings of the banking crisis were in place. To put the matter in perspective, if a firm has debt of five times its gross cash flow its debt is considered junk. The US non-financial sector reached a collective ratio of 4¼–4½ times at the post-bubble peak in mid-2001, even after adding back assets taken off balance sheet into special purpose vehicles (Enron-style). That meant perhaps one-third of the firms were above five and therefore junk. For the Japanese non-financial sector to be collectively on nearly seven times was dire. The cure was seven years of deflation.

The remainder of the story is of how Japan has remained chronically short of demand, because of the violent restructuring needed to put right the acute financial imbalances. In effect, Japan Inc was bust: internally bust, vis-à-vis its bank and household creditors – the external side showed a plenitude of overseas assets. By 2004, jobs had fallen by ½% a year for seven years; average weekly/monthly pay was carved up even more, falling 1¼% on average each year for eight years to spring 2005. Two recessions, in 1998 and 2001, formed part of this. The increase in business cash flow was tremendous. Business saving moved up even further than before to 25% of GDP – not far short of twice the US rate of business saving (which is itself quite strong). In cash terms, the money saved was not spent in any way but was used to repay debt: this was brutal debt deflation. In accounting terms, the major gains in operating profits were wiped out by provisions for depleted pension funds and losses on real estate holdings and cross-holdings of shares – much of Japanese business being plagued by old collectivist mutual ownership, cross-shareholding arrangements. By 2002, the worst was over and the economy started a good recovery, though labour incomes did not benefit for years, as we have seen.

Table 3 **Japan: structure of flows of funds, 2002, % of GDP**

	Saving	Investment	Balance
Households	3	3½	–½
Business	25	13	12
Private sector	28	16½	11½
Government	–	–	–8
Foreigners[a]	–	–	–3

a Current-account balance, sign reversed.

What happened next illustrates how one problem knocks on to another, and bad periods in a country's economic life can only be turned around with great difficulty. The structure of the flows of funds by 2002, at the start of the recovery is shown in Table 3 (bearing in mind that these flows have to add up to zero – one person's lending being another person's borrowing).

The structural savings glut was a massive 11½% of GDP even with a lot of wasteful business investment. (The balances in Table 3 do not add up precisely, owing to normal estimation errors.) But only one-third of that 11½% of GDP showed up as current-account surplus (foreigners' deficit) as two-thirds was absorbed by the government deficit, including the (largely wasteful) state capital spending orgy – the famous 'bridges to nowhere', 'vegetable airports', not to say 'paving Mount Fuji', all benefiting the iron triangle.

In the six years to 2008, the Ministry of Finance conducted an aggressive exit strategy (as we would now call it) from the high rate of fiscal stimulus (8% of GDP) that had been necessitated by the triple recessions of the previous decade. This deficit claw-back saw the government deficit cut to 2½% of GDP by 2007. Partly, this reflected the growth of the economy that took it from significant slack in 2002 at the end of the recession to an above-trend level of GDP in 2007. Whereas the total government deficit came down from 8% to 2½%, the cyclically corrected or structural (or policy) balance went from a 7% deficit in 2002 to a 3½% deficit in 2007. This was, nonetheless, seriously deflation-ary fiscal budgeting over five years.

The normal pattern for policy is that a balanced policy in a country with reasonable stability will offset fiscal rigour with monetary ease, or vice versa. Japan in 2002–07 was severely constraining domestic demand with fiscal rigour. The 3½% of GDP tightening of the structural budget was 0.7% a year and that figures large in a country whose potential growth rate is only about 1%, or at best 1½%. The policy reflex, given price deflation inherited from the long night of the nineties, was to offset this fiscal rigour with monetary ease, in the form of low interest rates. The zero interest rate policy (ZIRP) was only modified to raise rates to ¼% in mid-2006 and ½% in spring 2007, since when they have come down again to 0.1%.

But the reflex of low interest rates did nothing to stimulate domestic demand – quite the contrary. The strong finances of the private sector meant that little if any borrowing to invest was needed. But those same strong finances mean the assets of house-holds include bank balances that are some 1½ times GDP and 250% of their disposable income. (The comparable US ratio to disposable income is under 70%.) On these deposits, as a result of low interest rates, they receive no interest. So the low-interest-rate policy worsened the deflation of domestic demand arising from the fiscal tightening by depriving households of the interest income they might reasonably have expected in a growth period.

Where low interest rates did stimulate demand and growth

was in exports. The mechanism was the famous 'yen-carry'. Zero interest rates make yen a useful funding source for any high-yield asset – and also nil-yield assets such as commodity futures, whose cost of carry can destroy a position if they have to be financed at a significant interest cost. The high-yield assets went up as a result, vis-à-vis the yen, so yen-carry positions led to capital gains as well as positive income. The yen stayed cheap, at 120 per dollar, until the crisis struck in mid-2007. As well as the world trade boom centred on nearby China, Japan thus had cost advantages that helped its exports shift from 11% of GDP in 2002 to 16½% just before the crash, measured at constant prices. Net exports went up from 1½% to 5½% of GDP. Out of the total real gain over five years in GDP plus imports (that is, total supply and demand in the economy), half came from exports, despite their starting at only 10% of GDP plus imports. The gain of real net exports was two-fifths of the gain in real GDP.

Despite this major 4% of GDP gain in real net trade, the current-account balance only shifted up from 3% to 4¾% of GDP, as export prices dwindled with deflation and import prices rose rapidly in the commodity price boom. But a current-account surplus of just under 5% of GDP, combined with a government deficit cut to 2½%, means the private surplus was down to just over 7% of GDP from 11½% in 2002. The corresponding flows for 2007 are shown in Table 4.

While household and business saving were down a little, and housing investment up, the largest contribution to this drop in the private net saving balance came from more business investment. As this ratio has remained significantly higher than in the US, despite Japan's feeble growth, this can only be regarded as wasteful.

Table 4 **Japan: structure of flows of funds, 2007, % of GDP**

	Saving	Investment	Balance
Households	2	4	–2
Business	25	16	9
Private sector	27	20	7
Government	–	–	–2½
Foreigners[a]	–	–	–5

a Current-account balance, sign reversed.

Japan's fiscal exit strategy has proved a complete failure in the context of the credit crunch and crisis. Fiscal and monetary policies made the country entirely dependent on export growth and wasteful business investment for growth. But the credit crunch caused all the yen-carry borrowers to abandon their positions and scurry for cover. They therefore repaid their funding, driving up the yen. Japanese investors running for cover drove it up more as they repatriated funds from exotic locations. Japan got sharply less competitive just as world trade collapsed. The 40% drop in Japan's export volume squeezed profits drastically and business investment was shredded. The recession of 8½% over four quarters was the worst among the G7 economies. Comparing Japan's end-2009 GDP with end-2001 GDP – a cyclically fair comparison of economies at the end of two recessions – it increased by 6% over the eight years. This was better than Germany's feeble 3½%, let alone Italy's disastrous –¼%, but still less than 1% a year – worse even than in the nasty 1990s.

Can Japan recover, beyond the technical snap-back in inventory behaviour after the extreme liquidation at the worst of the recession? The outlook is not at all promising. Because of the recession, 2010 forecast government deficits – 8% actual and 7%

structural – are back to 2002 levels. Government debt is 100% net of offsetting financial assets, 200% gross. These already mountainous public debt levels must constrain any attempt at Keynesian budget stimulus, especially with deficits already back to extremely high levels. The financing for those deficits is there for the time being, of course – where else can the bulk of Japanese citizens' private surplus go? (The collapse of business investment has sent the private financial surplus back up to 11% of GDP.)

But policy freedom is almost completely lost. Fiscal stimulus is out. Interest rates are already nil and cannot go lower. The yen is strong. Worse still, deflation is taking a lurch for the worse in Japan. To analyse what may happen in Japan, it is important to look at the distribution of income between the personal and business sectors. Consider the ratio of personal disposable income to GDP:

- US   78%
- Germany   65%
- France   65%
- Japan   59%

We know that the US ratio is too high as it is supported by government and current-account deficits that cannot be sustained in the long run. The ratios for Germany and France look on the low side, but as well as supporting the business sector the rest of GDP (or gross domestic incomes) has to support a large, European-style public sector. In Japan, however, the public sector is similar in size to that in the US, and far smaller than in Europe, and yet the personal-sector disposable income is fully 6% of GDP (one-tenth of the roughly 60% magnitude) less than Germany and

Figure 32 **Japanese jobs and average wages**
%, latest 12 months vs. previous 12

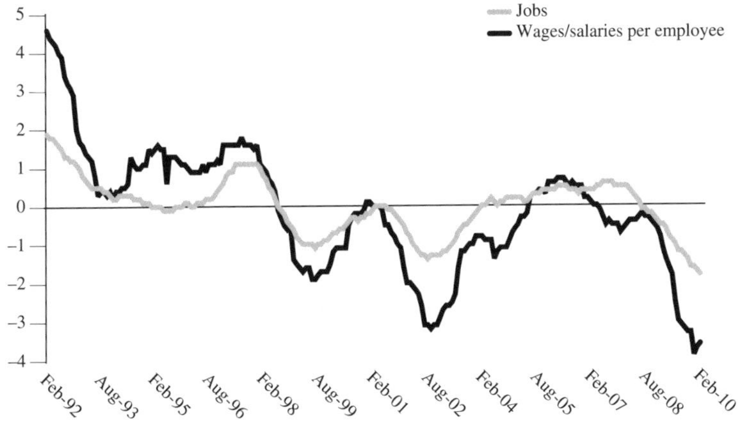

Source: Japanese Department of Employment

France. So Japan's basic problem, in relation to its failure to generate sufficient consumption, is simple: the business sector hogs too much of the national income.

Yet the response to the current crisis has been for Japan to cut labour income drastically, increasing the distorted excess of the business share of income. As Figure 31 shows, we have reached the point where jobs are falling by over 1½% a year and weekly pay by more than 3½%. So total labour income is falling at 5–5½%. Meanwhile, deflation is naturally intensifying: weekly pay falling at 3½% combined with underlying productivity gains of perhaps 1% mean that unit labour costs are falling at 4½%. But deflation of consumer prices on the broadest definition (the deflator for consumer spending in the national accounts) is 'only' 2½%. Two things follow. First, real, price-adjusted income of labour is falling, owing to the 2½% difference between price deflation and the rate of shrinkage of nominal labour income. Second, deflation of prices could intensify as unit labour costs are falling faster, even though the business sector is happy to grab an even larger share of overall income in the meantime.

A problem that does not exist is how to get Japanese households to consume. The savings rate of 3% is already low, suggesting that the Japanese are willing to spend money, once they have it (in contrast with the Germans, for example). Furthermore, retired people tend to spend all their income, whereas late-career income is heavily saved. The large 1930s generation's retirement has already lowered the savings rate, but the retirement of the baby-boomers (born from 1950) should lower the savings rate even more. So with nominal wealth of more than seven times disposable income, the business sector hogging cash flow and government debt looking less and less attractive to hold, it is conceivable that once the baby-boomers have retired, the Japanese population will consume capital – that is, reduce its saving rate below zero, consuming more than 100% of disposable income.

The shrinkage of labour income poses a double problem for policy: how to deal with collapsing real consumer incomes that, as the personal savings rate is already low, could hammer consumer spending; and how to prise a large chunk of total income in the economy out of business and into personal income.

The two policy problems are aggravated by a major social change that has taken place over the past 15 years: the end of the lifetime employment system. Under this paternalistic system until the mid-1990s, firms provided a complete social-security network for their employees, including, often, housing as well as health and pension benefits, and involving the payment of substantial bonuses on top of regular wages in the months of June,

July and December. But criticisms of Japan's rigid supply side and its fixation on turnover rather than profit, combined with the corporate debt crisis of the mid-1990s, induced firms to behave in a more market-oriented way. This did not lead to more competition or less profit-gouging. On the contrary, the imperative of debt reduction led to increased profitability by ensuring that new employees were not hired on lifetime-employment terms, but on the sort of arm's-length terms that are common in America. After more than a decade of much reduced adherence to lifetime employment, the proportion of the labour force employed on such terms has gone down a long way. More than one-third of employees are now on temporary contracts. As the baby-boomers reach retirement age, this trend will accelerate.

In the recent crisis, the shrinkage of profit margins was severe as exports fell 40% by volume. So yet again, cutting labour costs wherever possible became a priority. So far Japanese consumption has held up well considering the pressure on labour income. But this is likely to have meant further falls in an already small savings rate. The natural thing to hope would be that income will be boosted by the improvement of profits. But as rising rates are not on the horizon, interest income is likely to remain minimal; and dividends are unlikely to increase. Stockmarket pundits are forecasting a jump in after-tax profits, perhaps by as much as half. But nobody is supposing this will lead to a higher dividend payout. Retentive corporate Japan will simply hold onto the money.

The natural response to this corporate behaviour is to recommend that the tax on company profits paid out as dividends should be nil (or minimal) but the tax on retained profits should be punitive. This might help, but it does not get to the heart of the problem. The snag, as pointed out by Andrew Smithers, is that much of the cash flow in Japanese business is depreciation, tax-free by definition, whatever the tax rate on pre-tax profit, as depreciation is a tax-deductible expense. Depreciation in Japan is 21% of GDP, compared with 15% in Germany, 14% in France, 13% in the US and 12% in Britain. This huge flow of cash cannot be touched by conventional measures. The government could make it taxable by enforcing a huge write-down of depreciable assets – they are so large because of uneconomic overinvestment in the past, so writing down their value is probably realistic – and then disallowing the loss from use in future years: that is, no tax loss carry-forwards. But this would be a drastic invasion of private property rights and is unlikely to happen.

So the conclusion has to be that the needed revival of Japan's economy by consumer spending will not happen in the next few years through policy changes. The 1% growth rate of the 1990s – regarded as such a feeble performance at the time – gave way to even worse in the cycle from end-2001 to end-2009. Nor is any improvement on the horizon. On the contrary, the recession could easily revive as a 'double-dip' in the next year or two and the downward spiral of the economy reassert itself, alongside the downward spiral of deflation.

Ironically, Japan's much-discussed demographic decline may prove more a help than a hindrance. The demographic risk is that the future will require the working part of the population and its capital to support much larger burdens than in the past, owing to the much increased ratio of older, retired people and the low rate of reproduction. Expressed in financial terms, this is like saying that the obligation to pay pensions to future pensioners is a much larger ratio to national income than has been true in the past. Add to this a huge pile of government debt inherited from battling the 20-year torpor – or, put another way, combating excessive private savings – and the resources available for active members of the population could be curtailed. But of course the reduced ratio of such active people will give them greater bargaining power in offering their labour, leading in normal economic logic to higher, not lower, real wage and salary incomes.

The result should at some stage be high real incomes for working people, who are in short supply, but less for the numerous pensioners. This could occur directly, through inadequate resources to pay pensions and shrinking profit incomes as a result of high real labour pay; and indirectly, as extra taxes levied by government to finance pensioners, who would use their voting power, cut into the flow of funds that normally go into interest and dividend payments. How does the ageing problem interact with the huge debt run-up used to counter the private savings excess? The hope must be that older Japanese, confronted with falling real incomes, start to liquidate their capital.

The ageing of the baby-boomers, currently in high-saving late career, might be a cause for optimism in Japan, in the absence of action to get cash out of the business sector. Already, the ageing of the large generation born in the 1930s has helped take net household savings down from 14–15% of disposable income at the beginning of the 1990s (end of bubble) to 10% by the turn of the century and 2–3% now. Baby-boomers are unlikely to retire young in Japan, where shifting to lower pressure work is more normal than outright retirement at, say, 65. But from 2015 onwards, some fallback onto income from savings is likely.

On present form, though real interest rates are quite high, real-isation of that implied purchasing power requires recognising the role of falling prices by liquidation of assets, especially where they are interest-bearing. For example, with a 1% interest rate on government debt, but a 2% real boost to that return via consumer price deflation (while the nominal value of the debt remains unchanged), the real interest rate is 3%. But a pensioner would have to liquidate 2% of his or her investment each year to get this full 3% value in consumption. This deters people from spending, as asset liquidation is generally supposed to go against the grain of a high-saving, cautious people. But shortage of labour once the baby-boomers retire could finally create upward pressure on wages, so that older people might feel less compunction about consuming the results of a lifetime of hard work and national post-second-world-war recovery.

It is entirely possible that the savings rate could become negative, given the prospective preponderance in the population of old people with large assets. If so, Japan might eventually, in ten years' time, recover. The huge nominal wealth of its people could finally start to be deployed in real spending. A useful public policy might be punitive death duties. Assets would have to be liquidated as annuities in order to avoid their loss at death. But such a drastic step is unlikely in consensus Japan.

9

Government debt spirals up

Japan explores the limits of government debt

A great 19th-century chess player, Siegbert Tarrasch, told by someone that his opponent had a 'won end-game', replied: 'Before the end-game, there is the middle-game.' He went on to win, of course. Before the long term, in which Japan may finally recover, lies the medium term – years 2–8, let us say – in which Japan is thought likely by many to go bankrupt, sunk by the upward spiral of already huge government indebtedness. Such concerns are not confined to Japan, with the chief deficit countries in the recent debt crisis, the US and the UK, running annual budget deficits well over 10% of GDP.

In this chapter the government debt burden of Japan, the US and the UK will be analysed in the context of the private sector's debts, its financial strength in terms of assets and net flows of saving and investment, and global exposures. My original exposition of the savings-glut idea anticipated the government balance sheet as the ultimate one to be trashed by excess savings flows from the Eurasian glut countries. The idea was that the domestic US deficits corresponding to the current-account deficit – that is, savings-glut countries' surpluses – were shifting. Borne by the business sector in the 1999–2000 bubble, the excess borrowing had shifted to the household sector in 2002–07, to be followed by the burden falling on the government once the household balance sheets had collapsed. So it has proved, though the crash took longer to come than was anticipated at the end of 2004 – and was worse as a result.

Table 5 **Debt, 2007, % of GDP**

	Net government	Gross government	Government + private non-financial (gross)	Gross total incl financial	Gross private non-financial + net government
Japan	80	167	333	440	246
UK	29	47	261	488	243
US	42	62	225	340	205
Germany	43	65	192	265	170

The Japanese government's net debt at the end of 2009 was around 100% of GDP and its gross debt 200% of GDP. These are extremely high levels and they are increasing fast: the numbers were 80% and 167%, respectively, in 2007, as Table 5 shows. With the rest of the world beginning to be like a globalised Japan in important ways, Table 5 shows that it is as important to look at total debt as at government debt. Japan's condition for the past 20 years led to the shifting of debt into the public sector, as well as an increase in the national total, once the private debt bubble burst, as it now has worldwide.

Crucial questions about the financeability of the debt concern the distribution of continuing deficits, the asset position of the household sector and the nation generally, the current flows of saving and investment and therefore sector financial balances, the rate of interest, and the effects of inflation or deflation. But the first thing to note is that gross debt, the commonly used criterion, overstates the problem of government debt, particularly in Japan, where net debt is only about half gross debt. To take the most obvious example, 20% of GDP is held by the government as foreign-exchange reserves, financed by gross government debt, but hardly a liability for Japan. Other matching financial assets are mostly domestic. But the net debt is clearly the right measure of Japanese government debt now that these financial assets are no longer valued on the bubble basis, that having burst in the 1990s.

In considering sustainability of total domestic sector debt, financial debt should be left out of account, except where bubble conditions mean government bail-outs are needed. In normal conditions, financial sector debt is entirely matched with, or outweighed by, offsetting financial assets. Thus in Table 5, Japanese financial sector debt is irrelevant. But end-2007 financial sector debt in the US and Britain, and to a lesser extent Germany, represents a potential burden on government, as the crisis revealed. If we treat a conservative 15% of financial sector debt in the US and Britain, and half of that ratio in Germany, as potential losses, and thus an implicit addition to net government debt, the totals from the last column would be representative of the true debt burden on each economy. This gives rise to the revised Table 6.

In Table 6, Japan's total debt in 2007 was similar that of the US and less than the UK's. The two Anglo-Saxon economies are going through the process of shifting private debt to the public sector, the road Japan has trodden for the past 20 years. But suppose we are entering an era of no inflation, probably deflation, as the argument in this book suggests. Then with real government bond yields and interest rates in the 2–2½% region (less

Table 6 **Debt and wealth ratios to GDP, 2007, %**

	Net government with financial debt adjustment	Household	Non-financial business	Total	Household financial wealth net of non-mortgage debt	Net wealth as multiple of non-household debt
Japan	80.4	62.1	88.6	231.2	257.5	1.52
US	58.3	95.9	80.4	234.6	334.6	2.41
UK	62.8	108.8	100.6	272.2	281.6	1.72
Germany	39.5	63.5	63.2	166.2	169.3	1.65

for short-term paper, more for long-term) and private rates higher than this, a real interest-rate assumption for the whole economy is about 4%, meaning that Britain's debt in Table 6 costs 11% of GDP, Japan's and America's 9% and Germany's 6–7% (perhaps rounded down, given the implication of a superior national credit rating). These numbers are challenging, but not crippling, and the different elements of debt, government, household and business bear upon different income flows in the economy, so the analysis will be complex.

Before moving from the real to the nominal – a highly relevant shift in Japan's deflationary case – the asset position of the household sector must be considered. For this, housing assets and mortgage debt will be ignored, as they are not relevant to holdings of financial assets that could include government debt: mortgage debt is financed out of wage and salary income, not by investment income. (Also, of course, their valuations have moved all over the place in recent years.) On this basis, net financial assets of Japanese households in 2007 were 270% of GDP, whereas government net debt was 80% and business gross debt another 90% of GDP, making a total of 170%. So relevant Japanese household assets are more than 1½ times the combined net government debt and gross business debt. Of the difference (100% of GDP), household holdings of equities accounted for less than one-third, so their decline since 2007 leaves the debt more than fully covered. This reflects the fact that over the past 20 years government deficits have been in response to a savings glut in Japan, so the asset build-up has naturally ended up exceeding the debts incurred.

When it comes to financial flows, Japan's private-sector excess of savings over investment is back over 10%. So although the current-account surplus has fallen from 5% of GDP in 2007 to 2½–3% after the export-led recession, it is no surprise that the government deficit is only about three-quarters of the private financial surplus. Here again, as with the private asset coverage, a debt crisis in Japan is hard to establish.

Clearly, Japanese government debt is growing. Relative to GDP it is raised not only by the addition of each year's deficit, but also by the effect of deflation; as deflation is now greater than real economic growth, nominal GDP is falling. However, the same deflation is swelling household and other financial asset holdings relative to GDP, so deflation does not stop Japan's debt problem being an internal matter for its citizens, rather than some potential global financial snare. Deflation has the effect of understating the private financial surplus and the government deficit. This is most obvious for the latter, as an example will show. With nominal interest rates on Japan's government debt of 1%, deflation of 2%, and therefore real rates of 3%, the charge to the budget each year is only one-third of the true, real interest cost. But likewise for households on the plus side, their bank accounts yield no interest, but nonetheless gain in real value each year by 2% in this example. And those accounts are no mean matter, including bank deposits amounting to 150% of GDP, half as much again as the net government debt.

In the Japanese context at least – that of private-sector financial surplus – deflation clearly makes a high government debt more sustainable, contrary to popular folklore. The general point is that inflation sharply increases the immediate debt-service burden and makes long-duration debt impossible. For example, with (say) 10% inflation and a 3% real interest rate, a government (or any other) borrower will in year one effectively repay 10% of the principal (plus anything in the loan terms). So obviously inflation is reducing the real value of the debt: it is forcing early repayment. This forced amortisation makes long-duration debt impossible. For example, whereas with zero inflation a perpetual bond like the British War Loan is truly infinite in duration, with 10% inflation, and a drop of its price to raise the yield by ten percentage points, half the principal put up by a buyer at this new, lower price has effectively been paid back in just over four years.

So inflation does indeed reduce the value of debt outstanding. In the late 1960s and early 1970s, the acceleration of inflation came as a surprise to most people. As a result, real interest rates were lower than normal, as nominal rates were too low relative to the inflation that actually occurred. In that situation, accelerating, unexpected inflation did indeed bail out debtors and penalise lenders. Bond market vigilantes have had scarred memories ever since. But an inflation shock is precisely what we are not getting now; on the contrary, a deflation shock is probable. The vigilantes going on about (non-existent) inflation have helped raise real (US and UK) government bond yields to unusually high levels, adding to the headwinds curbing the recovery. Since markets are not caught out by inflation, it is reflected in the burden of high nominal interest rates – and the impossibility of long duration (other than with inflation-indexed bonds) is a severe constraint.

The placidity of the Japanese government bond market proves the point. Even with net debt at 100% of GDP, the net burden of interest is only 1% of GDP – scarcely crippling. So the question becomes whether this is a primrose path to ever-rising debt and some ghastly future denouement. The prospect of real household holdings of government paper – which boils down to claims on taxpayers, in other words themselves – mounting without end in tandem with the national debt is certainly alarming. If the upward spiral is not broken in some fashion at some point, eventually consensual 'disarmament' could become necessary. In other words, write-offs – or defaults, to put it rudely. And the process by which that might happen could never be pretty.

The likely scenario is that once the baby-boomers retire they will eat into their capital. Ironically, while this would be the beginning of a cure for the Japanese malaise, it would mark the point at which financial problems would finally arise from the heavy government debt burden. As soon as households start to liquidate their capital, with the savings rate significantly negative, the economy should recover and interest rates should rise, forcing the government's hand over its deficit. But a rise in interest rates would add to personal income, owing to the huge sums on deposit. This would add to the upward impulse to the economy, and mandate an exit from budget deficits. The problem with the exit of 2004–07 was that it was based purely on export demand as the source of growth. A durable recovery of domestic consumption would be quite another matter.

As to timing, the sort of recovery being discussed here is unlikely within five years, though it should be starting within ten. The question becomes whether the net government debt can blithely be taken up from the current 100% of GDP to what could be close to 200% in ten years' time. Improbable though such an idea is it is hard to see what might cause a crisis. But while we could reasonably conclude that Japan would get away with it, the rest of the world is unlikely to leave Japan to work through this scenario in peace, as the rest of this book suggests.

Anglo-Saxon government debt to soar

The current policies of the US and UK governments mean that their debt is starting to climb as Japan's did nearly 20 years ago. Important questions are how quickly the private sector's finances are being rectified by debt pay-down and what an eventual equilibrium rate of private-sector flows might be. Both countries, even after the asset price falls of the past two years, have household asset coverage of (adjusted) net government debt and gross business debt about equal to Japan's 1½ times. But each has a higher ratio of household investment in the stockmarket, even after the crash and partial recovery. This reflects the negative net asset position of the Anglo-Saxons vis-à-vis the rest of the world, in contrast to Japan's surplus – such are the results of decades of mounting global imbalances. Foreign ownership of government debt is large in both countries, and is reflected in government paper, with 50% of US Treasuries and 30% of British government gilts owned abroad. This is the chief source of their vulnerability, compared with Japan.

US private-sector debt needs to come down to 150% of GDP (75–80% for households, 70–75% for business) from its peak of about 180% of GDP (see Chapter 2). If its current 7% of GDP private-sector financial surplus (gross savings minus gross investment) were entirely devoted to that purpose, the process would take about four years. But much of the financial surplus will be diverted to other purposes. Corporate America has almost all the private sector's surplus, and does not exist to buy government bonds. But it was cutting debt by issuing equity at a rate of 2–2½% of GDP in 2008–09, some of which was bought by foreigners. And while price inflation could sink to zero by the end of 2010 or early 2011, strongly falling prices are unlikely. With modest real growth in prospect, GDP could gain at least a nominal 10% over five years, and that by itself would cut the private debt ratio from 180% to 164%. So it seems reasonable to assess the debt adjustment period as five years or less. Before the end of that period, the private-sector surplus should be coming down from its current 7% of GDP, though not for a couple of years as the household savings rate is still far below the 7–8% of disposable income that is its probable medium-term destiny.

The US government deficit, currently 10% of GDP, is larger than the private surplus by the amount of the current-account deficit, currently some 3½% of GDP. The policies of the chief savings-glut countries are either reverting to export-led growth (China) or likely to cause an import-reducing recession (Japan and Germany). So the US deficit seems only likely to shrink slowly as the probable slump in commodity prices resulting from continued weak demand eases the import bill. The prospect is that US government borrowing could average not far short of the current 10% of GDP for five years. In that case net debt could mount to 90–100% of GDP, compared with 42% in 2007 and 56% in 2009.

What is a likely long-run equilibrium level for private financial balances? Household saving needs to be 5–6% of GDP (7–8% of disposable income) or close to that. Housing investment, now down to 2½% of GDP, need not revive much for the foreseeable future. So the balance of these two could be 2–3% positive. On the business side, the 2002–07 financial surpluses were in the region of 3% of GDP. But this was a period of rebuilding of business balance sheets after ruinous behaviour in the 1998–2000 bubble, followed by recession. In future, profitability could well come down somewhat, as the global excess supply of capital creates downward pressure on the return to capital (for capital as for other things, excess supply undermines price). Moreover, in due course businesses will have to boost investment from current levels that are below the rate of depreciation. So a longer-run neutral balance between business saving and investment could easily be only minimally positive (which is roughly the 50-year average).

These factors imply a positive balance of 3% for the private sector as a whole. With a current-account deficit of, say, 2% of GDP, the government deficit would be 5% of GDP. If nominal growth were 3%, the government debt ratio would head towards 160% (or 5/3, the deficit ratio divided by the nominal growth rate). If nominal growth were 5%, of course, the debt ratio would stabilise at 100%. This would appear to revive the idea that a little inflation helps with debt. But the deficit ratio could only be kept at such a posited 5% of GDP by cutting real spending to offset the higher nominal interest rates on existing debt that a return to inflation would entail.

The balance of the argument tends to the conclusion that continuation of current policies and behaviour patterns in the savings-glut countries will put the US in an intolerable position vis-à-vis its government debt burden for the long term. This effectively is a restatement of the earlier observation that the only sound way out of the global imbalances is action by savings-glut countries to stimulate their consumption – in other words, reduce their savings glut. The US needs to move to current-account balance or surplus to achieve reasonable growth, adequate personal savings to permit baby-boomers eventually to retire and stable, if too high, government debt.

Britain is adjusting more violently than the US. It needs to. Whereas US non-financial private-sector debt was 180% of GDP in 2007, Britain's was 210%. The gap to be narrowed to cut it to 150% would be twice as large. But British households can bear more debt than their US counterparts as the debt in question includes unincorporated business debt – included in business debt in the US – and the spending habits of British households are less lavish, leaving more scope for meeting interest payments on mortgages. On the business side, British gross debt levels are partly offset by more corporate cash than in the US, so that affordable debt is also probably higher.

Whereas the US private-sector financial surplus is currently running at 7% of GDP, Britain's is close to 10%. With a current-account deficit of 1–2%, the budget deficit totals 11% of GDP. Apart from the private surplus suggesting Britain may eliminate its excess of private debt faster than the US, the current account is also likely to be a more favourable factor, as Britain has a free currency – unlike the dollar, whose chief exchange rate is set in China. From a lower level of net government debt than the US in 2007, Britain is likely to see it rise to a similar 90–100% by 2015.

The long-run surplus of the household sector (British-style, including unincorporated business) should be some 2% of GDP, comprising 9% gross saving (6% pure saving plus 3% unincorporated business depreciation) and 7% gross investment (4% for unincorporated business plus 3% for housing). In recent years, as in the US, the corporate sector has been in healthy surplus, but this is likely to go away (again as in the US). Over the past 20 years, the corporate sector has averaged a roughly zero balance. As the descent of the pound should improve the current account towards balance from its (quite small) deficit, the prospective government deficit to balance these factors could be half the US projected 5%, that is, 2–3% of GDP. This is consistent with stable (if high) government debt levels if growth is 2% and inflation, owing to the weakening exchange rate, remains positive (unlike in the US). So the British projection, while a cause for anxiety, especially in the short term, does not look like a structural crisis in the same way that America's does.

The short-term risks in the British debt position are a reminder of the 1976 sterling debacle, but are unlikely to turn out so drastically. The point is that the start of recovery involves an inventory snap-back that significantly shrinks the financial surplus of the business sector, part of which (at the trough of a recession) arises from liquidating inventory. That shrinkage of the counterpart surplus leaves the government deficit less easy to finance. This is exactly the position during 2010, with the business-sector surplus in at the end of 2009 at a remarkable 10% of GDP, and the current account temporarily returned to balance. The problem for the observer is that strong action to cut the government deficit would probably restore confidence and strengthen sterling, creating a double-whammy discouragement of recovery: tighter fiscal policy combined with appreciation of the currency. The new coalition government is particularly exposed to this risk as continental Europe, which takes half of Britain's exports, could be heading for depression. Assuming this government can sustain its austerity programme for a year or more, the danger of a sterling crisis is small. A much greater risk is that growth will be inadequate, provoking political instability, as action to cut the deficit may prove to have been too much, too soon.

10

What should be done and probably won't be

To see how the problems described here might be resolved, the issues of economic policy must be separated from those of financial governance and regulation. The latter have attracted most attention, partly because the crisis is widely (and wrongly) thought to have been primarily a financial crisis – a kind of Long Term Capital Management crisis writ large – and partly because regulatory issues (not to mention greed and fraud) are more easily understood and handled than the fundamental incompatibility of different countries' economic policy and behaviour.

In reality, renewed delinquent financial behaviour is something we have to worry about in the next 5–10 years only if the current economic and financial recovery progresses into a sustained growth period. In that case, with easy money having provoked the danger of a renewed bubble based on low interest rates, some of the recent 'back to 2007' behavioural trends could cause trouble. In the much more likely case that the world economy and financial system experience further major problems, the chastening of the banks will happen progressively in any case – strong changes in regulation will not be particularly important. But this erosion of the importance of the banks is also likely to happen even with a sustainable recovery.

One necessary condition of sustainable recovery is reduced debt ratios in the US, Britain, Spain, and so on. In that case, the volume of loans outstanding from banks is likely to be little changed, if not lower, in five years' time that it is now. And where the loans go, there go the associated derivatives, foreign-exchange hedges, swaps, and so forth. But with no increase of banking volume over five years, the only new loans will be rollovers of old ones. Far fewer bankers will be employed and banks will be less profitable (outside traditional investment banks' marketmaking and mergers activity), though lower profits will only come slowly as currently inadequate capital is rebuilt: the barriers to entry in banking – obtaining a deposit base and a licence – are high. So sustainable recovery scenarios almost inevitably imply a shrinking bank sector, with negligible risk of a repeat of 2005–06 behaviour, whatever is done about regulation. Suggestions about regulation are therefore important mostly for the 10–30 year future, not the next ten years, and are covered in Appendix 3. (Observe that the US Glass-Steagall Act, passed in 1933, did not become a significant constraint on banks until the 1970s.)

What are the broad priorities of the various countries that will drive their broad economic policies over the next 2–5 years?

- **America** needs to get its private non-financial debt down from the current 180% of GDP to 150%. It needs to make its growth and general economic development less dependent on conditions in the rest of the world, especially the savings-glut countries. It needs to reduce the rate of unemployment from the current near-10%. This set of goals is a tall order.
- **China** needs to reorient its economy to make consumption as well

as exports a primary source of demand (as in mature economies). Consumption now is secondary to, and depends on, exports and fixed investment, rather than the natural arrangement in which fixed investment is secondary to exports and consumption (which should be the primary purposes of any economy). This is a huge transition.

- **Japan** is in a parlous position (see Chapter 8) – but does it matter for the rest of the world? Its economy is large, but growth is negligible and imports small, relative to GDP. Nor are its potentially dubious government bonds much held abroad. So its fate does not have global economic significance.

- **Germany** needs to grow, rather than stagnate, and to devote a much greater share of the value it creates to its citizens' consumption and welfare. This should downplay secondary goals such as budget balance, let alone dubious political projects such as European political union that are not seriously supported by other countries' people or policies (whatever their leaders may say).

- **Britain**, like America, needs to cut its private financial debt without too drastic a rise in unemployment, but its capacity to make policy less dependent on the rest of the world is much less.

- **Club Med Europe** countries need to recover control over their economic policies. In particular, currency devaluation is essential to restore any possibility of future economic growth in Italy and Spain.

As will become clear, while all the countries and regions listed above face difficult times, the problems of the savings-glut countries are likely to prove much less tractable than those of the deficit countries, excluding Club Med, which is bound to suffer badly in extracting itself from the deeply destructive EMU. While China has catapulted itself into global prominence as a major economic power over the past 10–15 years, in the next few years the relative position of America is likely to strengthen, with China hitting some major economic teething problems.

Optimal Chinese policy and economic behaviour would probably be the best route to a healthy global recovery. Only through Chinese domestic expansion can the US enjoy, via strong exports, reasonably strong output and incomes growth while the share of consumption in output and income is cut by the needed increase in savings. But it is helpful to start the analysis from the traditional power centre of the US. It was US household debt that originated the crisis, and the US financial system that facilitated and encouraged the borrowing excesses. While a painful drying out is under way in much of deficit Europe – Club Med, the Atlantic isles, and central and eastern Europe – the US is the make-or-break deficit country for global balance-sheet adjustment and rectification of financial imbalances.

Equally importantly, the US is accustomed to lead – and expects to. Its natural activism means it will be tackling its problems as it sees them. Yet the argument in this book is that the fundamental economic cause of the imbalances, and hence of the debt excesses and crisis, was not the borrowers but the savings-glut, export-dependent surplus countries. It follows that whether they take action, either to reduce their savings glut or at least to ameliorate its malignant effect on others, is a crucial question for the world's economic future. So the US is in the unaccustomed position of heavy dependence on others for the key policies and behaviour affecting its economic future. This is bound to grate. Americans would much rather believe that the crisis arose from their blunders, their venality – their anything – rather than that they were essentially reactive, responding to conditions originating elsewhere that they were not well placed to influence.

That they themselves are to blame is what most American commentators believe, though they make a partial exception of China, and the yuan-dollar peg in particular. But this frame of mind is dangerous, not least because it is not true – or at least far from the whole truth. One effect of this is that failure of the surplus countries to take adequate action – and in good time – may precipitate US action that is likely to be a cure worse than the disease.

What are the makings of a healthy US recovery? This question concerns US balance sheets (especially household, more recently government, debt) and demand, not the supply side, which is in rude health. Indeed, the health of American business has con-tributed to the demand problem, as the fierce cost cutting in the recession was a major reason it was so deep. Private jobs and inventories were cut by 7–8% each and business capital spending by 20%. But business demand will return in force only if other elements of demand lead. Those other elements can only be:

- government-deficit driven, either state spending or tax cuts;
- consumer-led, implying a lower savings rate or at least no increase of it;
- net exports, either exports themselves or import substitution.

For a healthy recovery we can rule out extra government deficits – they are too large already. The second element, which implies continued inadequate consumer savings, is part of the debt problem, not part of any viable and sustainable solution. While falling household savings have re-emerged in the US recently, this is unlikely to last into the medium term, leaving net exports as the primary source of recovery. But a closer look at the first two elements will illustrate how the US recovery could soon disappoint those expecting a simple, traditional, V-shaped rebound.

Starting with government, US policy seems set to cut into growth, not enhance it. The state and localities mostly have balanced-budget laws, and the recession damaged their balances seriously, mostly by collapsing tax revenues. State and local spending moved down in real terms in the second half of 2009, and overall government spending, strong in the middle quarters when the fiscal package was being implemented, fell at the end of the year. While this had helped cut into state and local deficits by late 2009, continued austerity is likely at least throughout 2010 to get deficits under control and comply with the balanced-budget laws.

The US economy in early 2010 conveys an impression of strength that could last through the middle of the year, but is highly likely to fade later. The inventory snap-back had momentum through early 2010, as did exports to other countries rebounding somewhat from the recession (especially to commodity countries like Canada benefiting from the rapid Chinese economic rebound). But the dominant factor is quite simply that the rise in personal savings after the crisis went into reverse. From a low point of about 1% in early 2008, just as the economy was entering recession, the savings rate had risen to 3¾% a year later, and then 5.4% by the second quarter of 2009. But by late 2009 it was down below 4%, and in early 2010 it fell to 3%. The result has been a major contribution to growth from consumer spending, even though real income fell, as jobs declined and wage inflation slowed to a crawl.

This fall in savings is remarkable, as it is not driven, as before, by a run-up of debt-financed consumer spending. Back in 2006–07, when the saving rate was falling towards 1–2%, the increase of debt used to finance consumer spending – that is, beyond the amount financing physical investment in housing or purchases of extra financial assets – was in the region of 7–8% of personal disposable income. So the gross saving rate of households that were saving was this 7–8% plus the net 1–2%, which equals 8–10% of total household disposable income. That was the amount being put aside by the households that were doing the saving: the 7–8% of borrowing to finance consumption slashed it to only a 1–2% net savings rate. Now, however, household debt is falling. So the 3% net rate of saving is also the gross rate, which has therefore fallen drastically, by nearly two-thirds, from the previous 8–10% to 3%. This means that contributions to pension funds, repayment of mortgages via conventional level monthly payments, and so on, may in aggregate have become minimal.

Data for household acquisition of financial assets, which is not the same as gross saving in the sense used above, show spending of $700 billion in each of 2005 and 2006, rising to a peak of $1 trillion in 2007. This was followed by $600 billion in 2008 and $300 billion in 2009, giving an idea of the slowdown in gross saving of Americans since the crisis. Similarly, the value (at current prices, which are highly volatile) of net household assets was 6¼ times personal disposable income in mid-2007, just before the crisis. This crashed to 4¼ times in spring 2009 (the low point) and was 4¾ times at the end of 2009. This is close to the 50-year average of 4.8 times, but the 50-year average for the net savings rate is 7%, more than twice the recent 3–3¼%. Moreover, the 50-year average refers to a US population with a younger average age than today's, and in particular without the large baby-boomer generation getting close to retirement age. Yet these baby-boomers should be (and in most other countries are) in the high-saving late-career period of the life cycle.

The optimistic short-term scenario for US growth, in the absence of fast growth in exports – that is, strong consumption growth in savings-glut countries – revives the Chimerica synergy concept. US consumers carry on spending without saving, this time with even less gross saving (in the sense above). Business spending gradually revives as spare capacity shrinks. China willingly supplies cheap imports. Household debts get written down, without further damage to banks, as they have already provided reserves against such defaults. As a result, true household debt is less than the statisticians say it is, and further adjustment relative to income occurs as the latter increases, boosted by growth.

The difficulties of this scenario can be seen by looking at its effects on the flows of funds. It presumes no major budget cuts designed to reduce the policy deficit, as this would check the growth. As the total (including cyclical) deficit is 10% of GDP in 2010, and growth modestly above trend would cut the cyclical element by only two percentage points over a few years, the deficit could still be 6% in 2–3 years' time, with significant but not severe fiscal policy tightening. The household balance, now a little negative, could remain so. But the current-account deficit (that is, foreigners' surplus) would be increasing from the current 3½% in this scenario, to 5%, say (a modest estimate of what might happen). In this approach, treating the business sector as residual, its surplus would be down to 1–2% from the current 6½–7%. While such a cut would partly reflect higher business investment, it would also imply seriously reduced profitability. This could arise from strong appreciation of the dollar. Such a fall in profits and business cash flow would hurt the stockmarket and undermine the favourable wealth effect that is the primary driver of this growth scenario.

The numbers can be cut another way. Suppose the business surplus only fell to 4%, accounting for more than half of the 6% budget deficit. Then with a current-account deficit of 5%, the personal sector (the residual in this approach) would have to run into deficit of 3% of GDP – implying, with housing investment at about that level, that the personal savings rate has fallen to nil. In other words, the fall in savings to sustain this scenario probably has to be continual, not just the fall we have seen already down to 3% of disposable incomes. This is completely inconsistent with the rebuilding of household assets, and also (see below and Chapter 6) with the demographic trends arising from non-retirement of the baby-boomers.

Another re-jigging of the numbers gives unchanged savings at the current rate (that is, a small household sector deficit), the business surplus plausibly at 4% of GDP, and the current deficit (foreigners' surplus) at 5%. In that case, with the budget as residual this time, the deficit stays high at 8–9% of GDP, hardly improved at all from the current 10% rate. But as this is a good growth scenario, so the cyclical element in the deficit would be significantly reduced, such a deficit implies that the policy deficit has actually been loosened, not tightened. In other words, any cuts in badly placed states and localities are more than offset by a new federal fiscal stimulus. This is highly implausible.

Lastly, if the government deficit were cut to 6%, the business sector's surplus to 4%, with the personal sector in slight deficit, the residual would be the current-account deficit, which would be 2–3% of GDP – reduced from its current 3½%. But this is highly implausible, as the growth scenario proposed has already involved a boost to imports, and this would be bound to continue, causing the current deficit to be larger, not smaller. This wheels the numerical analysis round to the central point: a healthy US recovery with improved private-sector finances can be envisaged only if exports are growing fast. Only with fast growth of exports could any growth scenario coexist with a smaller current-account deficit.

What all these numbers say is that it is mathematically impossible to get the budget deficit down by a reasonable amount – by no means eliminated, just less grossly excessive – and simply hold household finances where they are (not rebuilding savings), and have an expanding economy in which growth of business capital spending is largely matched by improved profits, without a sharp further cut in the current-account deficit, if not its elimination. Such a lower net import figure cannot be conjured up in the revived Chimerica scenario. The numerical quandary, which drives towards the need for current-account equilibrium, becomes even more acute if a rebuilding of personal sector net wealth is posited.

Is this drop in household savings part of a drift into a new financial crisis? Certainly, it has been carrying the economy forward at an above-trend rate during early 2010. US households seem to be reverting partly to type – 'let's just go back to 2006' – and treating the crisis as a rude interruption, even if the former exuberance in borrowing can never be recovered. This is the spending counterpart of the so-called 'echo-bubble' in risk assets induced by zero interest rates and quantitative easing (QE).

Given the numerical constraints just detailed, what is likely to spoil the Chimerica scenario? One answer would be if the US decided – as advocated by the 'tea parties' – to cut sharply into the budget deficit. That would quickly take the steam out of the consumption-led recovery. Alternatives are monetary tightening by the Fed, the global impact of China's upcoming tightening, or random crises, most probably recession or depression in the euro zone. The Fed has already withdrawn QE. It could even start to sell back to the open market the more than $1 trillion of securities it has bought under QE. If the economy is seen as growing consistently faster than 3%, say, zero rates could also soon be abandoned. And the various levels of government, under strong political pressure from tea parties and others concerned about government deficits, might see such renewed economic growth as a chance to tighten budgets and cut deficits, even if not to the full satisfaction of the tea parties. These likely responses to the revived Chimerica scenario mean current above-trend growth is likely to subside quickly.

If these conditions imply no sustained strong domestic lead in the economy, either from government spending or from consumers, what of net exports? This breaks down into exports and imports, with the prospects for exports far from promising. The largest US markets are Canada, Mexico and Europe. But slower Chinese growth as 2010 draws on should slow growth in Canada and other commodity countries, dependent as they partly are on energy and metal industries. Meanwhile, the European economic shambles ensures there is little hope for US export growth in that quarter. Everywhere, the Chinese export juggernaut will curb other countries' market shares. So President Obama's declared goal of seeing US exports double in five years does not just look unachievable – 'cloud cuckoo-land' says it better. On the import side, prospects are brighter. As discussed above (Chapter 6), major import substitution has occurred over the past three years.

Given much better productivity performance than in most other advanced countries, though no longer a particularly competitive dollar exchange rate, domestic products may continue to gain market share from imports. But this is likely to provide only modest annual benefits to output from now on.

So of the three primary sources of demand, consumer spending will be growing, though probably more slowly than income, but output (and income) should be growing faster than total demand, owing to import substitution. Some back-up contribution from business investment can also be expected, as it is now only slightly higher than the depreciation rate (that is, capital assets are scarcely growing net of replacement). Businesses are highly profitable, so financing should not be a constraint.

A probable result is that the US economy will grow at or close to its trend rate or about 2½% over the next few years. It will not rebound with seriously above-trend growth over several years. The non-retirement of baby-boomers will increase the labour force unexpectedly fast, intensify deflationary pressures, hold unemployment high and help business profitability through downward pressure on wages. The higher savings rate as the still-working baby-boomers save their social-security cheques should mean output and income growth are not fully matched by consumption. As a result, the balance of payments could shift from deficit to equilibrium or even surplus. The US could well achieve a satisfactory reduction in private-sector debt and some lessening of dependence on the rest of the world for its economic well-being. But unemployment could stay stubbornly close to the current 10% level, which will be politically threatening. Dangerous policy lurches in response to this can be expected.

The likely shift downward of US net imports means the

savings-glut countries will have serious economic difficulties if they cannot find ways of stimulating domestic demand. They too will suffer in this scenario, even without US policy lashing out, though that seems entirely possible, even likely. The surplus countries, under their past and (mostly) current policies, remain dependent on export gains for growth. This in turn requires extra borrowing by deficit countries. As this is precluded in most of Europe, it means extra borrowing by the US and the UK. But that is exactly what will not be possible because of US economic developments and the British devaluation (which has helped sharply reduce net imports). Britain's prospects are similar to America's for much the same reasons. Britain has the advantage of a truly free-floating currency – the pound's main rate is not set in China, in contrast to the dollar. But it has the major disadvantage of half its exports going to an at best stagnant Europe, in an economy with much greater trade dependence than the US.

So if the savings-glut countries do not take action to raise their domestic consumption, the world is unlikely to recover much of the growth lost in the crisis, the Americans could get angry and the surplus countries themselves will underperform. This will mean a major cut in China's long-term growth rate, no growth at all in Germany and probable income degradation in Japan. A healthy recovery led by savings-glut countries requires either structural policies to lower excessive private-sector saving, or willing adoption of structural government deficits. Without this, the world could be facing a renewed economic downswing in a year or two, and a fresh crisis – this time not just financial and economic, but chiefly political. The issues have already become highly political, both along the US-Chinese axis of discontent and within Europe.

China chose in late 2009 to flex its political muscles and show the world its strength. The US, having got into the economic and financial crisis under the chauvinist Republican administration, had elected a more conciliatory Democrat, Barack Obama, in late 2008. China may have seen conciliation simply as weakness. In his trip to China in October 2009, in which he talked the language of economic and political co-operation, President Obama was set up by the Chinese leadership and made to lose face. Then in November, at the Copenhagen global-warming conclave, Chinese Premier Wen stayed away from an important meeting attended by Obama and numerous other world leaders at which some underling from China's foreign ministry berated America, and implicitly Obama. Wen followed that up by taking a strong public line against yuan appreciation as being effectively a foreign plot to put China at a disadvantage. In fact, it would be the single best immediate policy measure to improve the Chinese economy (see Chapter 5) as well as being highly desirable to rebalance the rest of the world, particularly the US, economy.

Chinese leaders do not have much international exposure. Perhaps they were unaware that 'dissing' the president of the United States without a good reason is bad policy, even if the US is perceived as weaker than it was. At any rate, they soon had the opportunity to learn. In short order, the US made large, highly publicised weapons sales to Taiwan and welcomed the Dalai Lama to the White House (having refused to do so in the mid-2009 conciliatory phase). The spat with Google has done China no favours either. More generally, conditions in China for foreign businesses are said to be getting less hospitable.

Several factors combine to reinforce the Chinese government's fixation on holding down the yuan's exchange rate. First, export industry success is the foundation of China's remarkable economic emergence, so it is natural to do everything possible to nurture it. Second, export industries have the money, and a powerful advocate in the Ministry of Commerce, so they dominate the smoke-filled rooms in which policy is hammered out. Third, the government consists of communists, educated from an early age to see capitalism as simple greed and economic life as a zero-sum game. So western appeals to let the yuan appreciate seem to them little more than a request to give the West some money. The idea of a win-win situation is not part of the communist mental framework. Lastly, yuan appreciation being what the West clearly wants, the natural thing for Chinese politicians to do is trade such a concession for something they want from the West. Against such considerations, the People's Bank of China's reasoned advocacy of yuan appreciation, or even flotation, is likely to win in the long term – the alternative still being real effective exchange rate appreciation, but via inflation. But it is relatively powerless until current policies cause China inflationary pain, as they will.

China will unquestionably have to allow the yuan to rise. Otherwise it will suffer major domestic trouble. Without significant yuan appreciation soon, the rapidly accelerating wage-price inflationary spiral will enforce strong domestic monetary restraint, undermining domestic demand and asset prices. This dilemma is already acute and bound to sharpen further. China could also lose some US access for its chief mode of economic development: exports. Recently, the US Congress has revived a proposal to place a large import surcharge on imports from China. This is one policy that the Republican opposition, adamantly hostile to President Obama's domestic initiatives, shows signs of supporting.

If adopted with bipartisan support, an import surcharge could become veto-proof: 60% congressional majorities are enough to override a presidential veto. China will no doubt react to this danger and reach a *modus vivendi* with the US. But yuan appreciation looks set to be little and late – almost certainly too little, too late. Certainly, overheating is past the point where domestic monetary restraint on some scale might be avoided.

This stand-off is the natural result of the reversion to type across the Pacific. Just as China has slid back into dependence on export-led growth, so the US is falling back on extra debt to ensure growth. But ultimately, the US, with a 10% government deficit to GDP ratio and little prospect of bringing it back within bounds over several years, is degrading its currency – even if there is deflation, and a strong dollar as other advanced countries look weak. Degradation will show in America's credit rating, just as Japan's credit rating and deflation is already reflected in its real ten-year bond yield of 3½%, well outside the normal range.

Yet the whole world's financial system depends on the soundness of US credit. That is what is at stake as the savings-glut countries jib at the challenge of expanding their consumption, rather than depending on exports. The eventual alternative to trashing US and other countries' credit could be that exporters' collective abuse of free trade leads to its being curtailed by protectionism. Any freedom withers if not used with responsibility – and that is just as true of free access to other countries' markets as any other freedom. Protectionism really would be a cure as bad as the disease. But it is certainly much worse, as the 1930s demonstrated, for the exporters than the importers. It would cause America to suffer some misallocation of resources and (finally) a risk of inflation. But the surplus countries would lose the chief motor of their economies, and would suffer drastic falls in growth rates. Medium-term economic decline could spread from Japan to the German-centred NCE, as well as from Italy to the rest of Club Med.

Before looking at the equally political issues arising from the European side of the global crisis, an alternative approach to equilibrium must be considered. This is a theoretical fantasy of how a workable medium-term outcome might be achieved even if savings-glut countries' growth continues to be excessively export-dependent. The idea is that the burden of their surpluses on deficit countries could be offset by two factors: steadily lower relative prices of their exports, lessening the real burden of imports on deficit countries; and a willing acceptance by the savings gluttons of low to negative real rates of return on the resultant net export surpluses.

This, however, is an inherently unlikely programme. As we have seen (Chapters 7 and 8), falling terms of trade have been part of the two-decade failure of Japan, where the yield of exports has plunged relative to imports, and also, more gently, of Germany, where the 20-year slope of the export/import price ratio has been $-\frac{1}{2}\%$ a year. So much for high-end Mercedes-Benz and BMWs – it would have been much more profitable to increase more rapidly the importance of high-end service industries. In China, the fundamental development impulse, competitive exports based on cheap labour, reinforced by the deliberately undervalued yuan, is designed to worsen the terms of trade over time. China's wastefulness in the use of metals and energy has contributed to excessive price upswings and further aggravated this trend through higher import prices.

In future, the decline in savings-glut countries' terms of trade could have to be faster. During the run-up to the crisis in the years to 2007, deficit countries were voluntarily raising their debt levels in the private sector. In future, their borrowing will be concentrated in the public sector, and acceptance of import growth will be under duress. The drop in surplus countries' export prices needed to make this acceptable to deficit countries would be correspondingly larger. Indeed, protectionism is simply an extreme version of such a fall in deficit countries' import prices: a tax on imports simply transfers part of their value from the exporting country/entity to the government of the importing country, reducing the value left with the exporter. (Part of the seductive charm of protectionism is that it can simultaneously raise revenue to offset deficit countries' budget deficits.)

When it comes to accepting a low to negative return on capital a similar pattern prevails: it has already been happening, but it could have to get worse. China has accepted a negative return on its savings by committing $2.4 trillion, half its GDP, to dollar reserves – with the dollar down against the yuan in the past and bound to be down further in future. That is what Germany has been doing with its implicit support, via the euro, for Club Med deficits, investment in overvalued Spanish houses, London real estate, American CDOs, and so forth. Here the Japanese, originators of the savings glut, have done less badly. Though Japan's dollar reserve build-up now totals 20% of GDP, its private investors have put much of the rest of the money abroad, and the Mrs Watanabes of this world – so-called night traders – have not done a bad job. But of course, the fundamental reality is that the destruction of wealth in the recent crisis has invalidated the wealth-accumulation rationale of all the savings gluttons. And so it will in future.

Surplus countries putting their net exports into deficit

countries' equities and real estate would be a valid alternative to accepting low to negative real returns. But leaving aside how poor the returns on such a strategy would have been over the past ten years or so, it would be psychologically at odds with the natural caution that underlies high savings in the first place. Chinese people who in 2007 stuck their toes in the water of international equity investment got them bitten off by barracudas in the crash. Outward investment through approved funds (QDII) has already been re-allowed, but it is likely to become a major factor only if the yuan is floated first, so that Chinese people are not spooked by the possibility that moving their funds abroad cuts them off from the benefit of future yuan appreciation. It is, however, certainly true that a bonfire of Chinese capital controls and a yuan float would, after an initial yuan jump, be a hugely positive move for global economic and financial adjustment. The problem is that it is highly unlikely.

Nor is the sale of the 'family' silver particularly welcome in the US, despite all the talk of free markets. Chinese and other purchasers have been denied access to key investments in recent years. Restrictions on foreign investors are manifold – in telecoms, airlines, other media, and so on – and likely to be reinforced if it were felt that China, in particular, were using an undervalued currency to grab market share and use the proceeds to buy up America. So this alternative equilibrium – continued imbalances with the surplus countries accepting worse terms of trade and negative returns on capital – is a false trail. It is highly unlikely to lead out of the imbalance jungle.

The elements of a globalised Japan are in place. Government debt is increasing, seemingly without limit, in response to the bursting of a private-debt-fuelled, asset-price bubble. Yet the onset of persistent deflation is in sight – only superficially a paradox alongside persistent deficits. And some five years of slower growth seem probable, that third element of Japan's long night of the 1990s (which seems to have returned after a brief 2004–07 respite). Slower growth could be concentrated in the Chinese portion of the Chimerican Siamese twins. In the much more difficult conditions of the next few years, with constrained world trade and a risk of protectionism, China's export surge cannot last long at the pace maintained in 2004–08, and its policy of extravagantly wasteful domestic investment is likely to cut into potential growth. The chief priority should be to develop a consumer-led, market-price-driven economy to replace the excessive emphasis on exports and investment. But relapsing into the comfort zone of export-led growth is the easier option actually being adopted. The huge task of adjusting China's economy to consumption-led growth (see Chapter 5) has yet to be even started; and it will depend for sufficient progress, if it ever does start, on the government accepting an unlikely relaxation of control over its citizens.

There is another catch. If China's exports are currently booming and America is reducing its import dependence through substitution, who is giving ground? World trade has recovered only some of the losses made between autumn 2008 and spring 2009. But China's export volume is back to 2008 peaks. To some extent this growth is at the expense of Pacific rim rivals, especially Japan. But many of them, South Korea and Taiwan for instance, as well as Japan, also gain from the Chinese export boom as they supply the parts for Chinese assembly plants. With Chinese exports strong and America importing less, the real losers are likely to be European businesses, in their share of both world exports and domestic markets, where Chinese inroads continue.

It may be too Machiavellian to look for a deep motive in China's pronouncements. But from early 2009 onwards, the People's Bank of China (PBOC), and even Premier Wen, was heard to complain about having to accept dollars in its reserves at ultra-low interest rates. Of course, the yuan's peg to the dollar means it has little choice but to accept dollars that leak through capital controls. The immediate effect of such a comment was to spur the dollar bears to bid up the yen and the euro. The resulting fall in the dollar, and thus the yuan, helped the increase in Chinese export competitiveness vis-à-vis Japan and Europe. So the European Central Bank and other Frankfurt-Berlin cheerleaders who egged on the inflation-obsessives with dire predictions of the dangers of policy stimulus have reaped their just reward: serious loss of competitiveness of European business. Game, set and match to the PBOC, as Chinese exports boom best.

The combination of violent deflation in Club Med, and Germany and other NCE countries set on budget balance – always leaning to deflationary policies – threatens continued recession in Europe bordering on depression. French domestic demand has been quite well sustained but cannot drag up the whole continental economy – indeed, shows signs of being dragged down by it. Nor will EMU get much benefit from recovery in the euro zone's largest export market, Britain. Devaluation of the pound has largely eliminated the British current-account deficit, measured in real terms; such extra demand as it has is not spilling over to the continent.

Even depression will not be enough to cut Club Med wages by 20% and make them competitive within the euro. So the condition for the euro to survive is fusion of euro-zone economies and countries into a political union. (Serious-minded Germans always said this was a precondition for a workable monetary union in the first place.) Under such a political union, the financial transfers from rich to poor that are needed could be effected, with policies, including eradication of Mediterranean governance habits, to attempt to ensure future Club Med competitiveness. However, the frequently cited model for such a federal system, the United States of America, only became the effective political and monetary union it is today by means of a civil war and the Great Depression. Maybe the euro-zone countries have the stomach for such a fusion. One doubts it and hopes not – the process would be very ugly.

Much more probably the euro zone will split up. What is inconceivable is that EMU can persist in its present form. Just as it ensures interest rates too low and exchange rates too high in Club Med, so it involves interest rates too high and exchange rates too low in Germany and surrounding countries. So the reality is that the depression of German consumption and the overcompetitiveness of its exports are closely linked to the subsidisation of real incomes and hopelessly uncompetitive labour costs in Club Med. But Germany has no real control over the disbursement of the subsidy and distribution of its income to Mediterranean consumers. For similar reasons, no monetary union in history has persisted without political fusion.

One logical outcome might be for Germany, France, Benelux and Austria to slough off Club Med. But such a clean break is unlikely. France is much more pragmatic about government deficits than Germany, not to say empirically Keynesian, and feels the weight of Germany's inevitably greater economic power – which would be enhanced further in a smaller, more cohesive monetary union. France is likely to use the coming intense distress of the

Club Med countries as a lever to counter Germany's power and destructive policies. So the split, when it comes – probably not until one or two more crises have been endured – could easily involve Germany splitting from the euro zone, no doubt with the Netherlands and Austria, and perhaps Belgium. The euro zone would then dissolve, as there is no reason for France and the Club Med countries to stay together.

The world economy is at the end of the beginning of the crisis. The 25-year boom of 1948–73 burnt out in inflation, which had been making the boom increasingly unhealthy, starting from the late 1960s' 'guns and butter' financing of the Vietnam war. It took two oil-inflationary crises and nine years before the foundations of sound recovery had been laid. After the 25-year boom of 1982–2007, this time burning out in excessive debt, we are only three years – and the first crisis – into a comparably tough patch.

The deflationary implications of the savings glut have not yet become fully obvious even to most economists, let alone key government authorities. The crucial contribution of excessive saving to global imbalances and of those imbalances to the crisis is still only acknowledged by a minority. The behaviour patterns of major players – dependence on exports in China, Japan and Germany, and on government debt-led growth in the US and the UK – have hardly yet been modified. Nor is it clear that the cure this time, as opposed to the 1980–82 Volcker-Reagan inflation cure, will be better than the disease. The last great era of globalisation ended in 1914. When the countryman contradicted Robert Frost's romantic view of an unsullied, wall-free countryside with 'Good fences make good neighbours', Frost deprecated his down-to-earth sentiment. But the countryman was realistic, and in the world economy globalisation has taken away the fences.

Resolution of current difficulties is almost certain to involve economic conflict, across the Pacific and in continental Europe. We have to hope this will not degenerate into outright war.

What does seem clear is that the coming adjustment period will be worse for the savings-glut countries than the non-EMU deficit countries. One reason for this is that the debt problems of the deficit countries are well understood. This permits, and in time will ensure, action to reduce the dependence of growth on fresh borrowing. But the crucial role of excessive saving in provoking the extremity of the debt orgy is not much understood, and little acknowledged. It follows that we are a long way from action in savings-glut countries to generate domestic consumption (not wasteful investment) and reduce dependence on exports – which are bound to be curtailed now that the deficit countries have to reduce borrowing.

When it comes to stimulation of consumption, Japan perhaps would but can't and Germany certainly could but won't. China is groping for a solution, but it has created an economy where consumption is dependent and secondary, the primary sources of demand being exports and investment. Both are taken to the point of wasting resources, generating assets and reserves with negative returns. Yet the key to making consumption an independent driver of the Chinese economy may be relaxation of government control over its citizens, and therefore conceptually impossible for China's current rulers. Compared with these obstacles, curbing the consumption of the Anglo-Saxon world and, via a lower real exchange rate, its net imports, seems a relatively straightforward, if painful, task.

Appendices

1

Mortgage-backed securities: the alphabet soup

The idea of a mortgage-backed security (MBS) was originally to lower the cost to households by cutting out the middleman: the bank lender in this case. Given the large volume of mortgages still being created that end up as MBSs after being sold to US government sponsored agencies such as the Federal National Mortgage Corporation (Fannie Mae), this continues to be the practice.

The basic concepts are simple. In the old days a bank would lend money for house purchase via a mortgage, for example with a 30-year repayment schedule. This involved some risk of the mortgage-taker defaulting at some stage over the 30 years. Suppose the bank took the same risk vis-à-vis a large number of householders. Provided they were roughly similar in characteristics (such as income or house price), these loans would default at about the average rate for such loans. Suppose 1% was the long-run average rate of loss from defaults. The bank would need to charge householders 1% more than its own cost of funds to justify the risk, plus a further margin, say 0.5%, to cover risk – that is, secure a good return on the equity base or reserves it would need to have in place to insure against the default experience turning out worse than normal. Suppose the bank was not rated AAA (the top rate – few are) but perhaps just A. (In between comes AA, traditionally a pretty low degree of risk.) Then the mortgage interest cost to the householders would be the A rate for 25 years plus rather over 1%: 1.5% in this example.

Level one: MBSs

The concept of an MBS is to remove the bank from this credit chain. In the late 1970s and 1980s, Wall Street moved into what had previously been a government-sponsored preserve (Fannie Mae and others) and started private-market MBSs. By the end of the 1980s, the previous debt-fuelled American boom had burnt itself out and added major domestic bad-debt problems to the banks' leftover wrecked assets resulting from the earlier Latin American overlending. By general consent, Citibank, for example, had it been wound up in 1990, would have proved insolvent. A Citibank bond issue might cost it significantly more than the A rate; together with its own on-lending margin in making a mortgage loan, this would add up to a major burden on the household borrower.

But banks like Citibank, the largest in America, do not like to be cut out of the mortgage business. The solution was to find a way of making mortgage advances that did not involve the interpolation of Citibank itself into the credit chain for 30 years. It needed to find a way of using its huge customer base in American households to continue to originate mortgages, but without expecting to hold onto the loans after they had been successfully set up.

Suppose a bank, for example Citibank, was borrowing at 1.5% over the risk-free rate (the rate at which the government borrows for 30 years). A rational bond investor could buy a bond secured directly on the mortgages for the same rate (1.5% over governments) and enjoy the same return as the bank, including the margin for equity risk. So it is likely to be profitable for the bank to lend to the householder not at the bank's borrowing rate plus 1.5%, but at its own borrowing rate – 1.5% over the government borrowing rate – and then put a sizeable batch of mortgage loans so generated into a separate company and sell them directly to investors, who will take them on board as readily as the bank's own paper. The securities set up in this way are known as mortgage-backed securities (MBS) or more generally asset-backed securities (as, later, the loans put into them could be other items such as auto loans, credit card receivables, and so on). The separate company is known as a special purpose vehicle (SPV – famous initials from asset-backed structures in the Enron case) or (more typically for 2000s mortgages) a structured investment vehicle (SIV).

The value of the 1.5% difference in borrowing cost from cutting out the bank's own balance sheet is large. For a loan of $100,000 over 30 years, with interest rates at 6%, a 1.5% interest differential has a present value of $16,500, one-sixth of the mortgage principal. A competitor bank could offer better terms to householders using this technique than a bank using its own balance sheet and still gain a portion of this value by selling the batch of loans to the SIV at a profit. Ultimately, competition forces down the cost of mortgages to householders to use up most of the present value from taking the bank out of the middle; but a portion remains to enable the loans to be packaged and sold in batches for a sum greater than their face value. This permits the bank to take origination fees and servicing fees (to gather the monthly payments, and so on) while releasing its capital and loan capacity for a new round of mortgages and fees.

Floating-rate MBSs

This is level one, the mortgage-backed vehicle, such as an SIV. In the last decade, with short-term interest rates mostly well below longer-term (such as 30-year) rates, the search for more affordable mortgages to extend the range and depth of the market has brought into prominence mortgage loans with rates that vary over time. (This is the normal structure in Britain and Spain.) The loan still has a long life, but the interest rate – and therefore the householder's monthly payment – is reset when short-term rates change. This structure (when packaged in an SIV) made possible periodic funding in the money markets, typically as commercial paper. Money-market investors might buy commercial paper with a short maturity, such as three months, secured on an SIV. If rates go up, the rates on the mortgages should rise to match the increased cost of funding, and vice versa.

How does SIV-backed commercial paper get repaid? By a new issue, of course. But what if the money markets decide they don't want that commercial paper any more? To guard against that risk, the SIV has a back-stop loan facility from the originating bank (or anyone else of suitable quality that wants to provide it). Meanwhile, as long as the SIV is out there in the market, funding itself with commercial paper, the mortgages are off the originator's balance sheet, and the usual fees have been taken early on to reflect the mortgage interest rate being somewhat above the rate demanded by the commercial paper investors.

Level two: CDOs – 'sliced and diced' MBSs

Level two is asset-backed securities themselves secured on the level-one SIVs, or other MBSs. MBSs set up with this approach to funding do not need to be funded in the bond or money markets as they are funded by the proceeds of second-level asset-backed securities, known as collateralised debt obligations (CDOs). The added value here arises from (for example) the investor appetite for high-grade, ideally AAA, securities and the dearth of AAA companies. If a batch of mortgages in an SIV can be expected on average to incur losses of 1% (the original premise above), it is a fair bet that a security having access to the first 95% of the cash flow is ultra-safe: 'as safe as houses' scarcely does it justice – this is safer than houses. If the normal recovery rate on the mortgages is 99% (face value of 100% less the 1% typical loss rate), what are the chances of failing to recover even 95%? Very small. A security that has first call on 95% of the cash flow is likely to be rated AAA.

Suppose that a high, AAA rating lowers the interest rate at which a bond can be issued by 0.5%. We have already seen that a saving of 1.5% has a present value of 16½% of the loan principal: one-third of that is worth more than 5½%. Add that profit to the 95% of face value involved and the deal has already yielded more than 100% of face value. The remaining 5% of the principal of the SIV – including practically all the risk – can be sold off at a discount and the whole deal is profitable. The SIV has been split into at least two second-level CDOs: the senior, AAA portion, and the junior rump. That rump was generally – to maximise the value of the deal – split into at least two pieces. The better part of it, limited to whatever amount of the principal (after the AAA first 95% in the example) that could be rated A or at worst BBB (at which levels it still counted as investment grade). This was known as the mezzanine tranche. The rest was known as the equity tranche, which, being virtually certain to be hit by proportionately large losses, has been nicknamed 'toxic waste'.

CDOs that were issued were a function of the ratings they were deemed to merit, that is, by rating agency models of the likely default rate. An AAA CDO could well contain the better portion of the risk from some good-quality mortgages, some low-quality mortgages, some asset-backed securities based on consumer credit – anything really, so long as it could be rated. The portion of the SIV or other asset-backed paper that could be declared AAA (or the mezzanine, A/BBB level) would depend on the expected default rate in the basic credit: mortgage, auto loan, or whatever. So the 95% used in the example above relates to good-quality mortgages. For lesser-quality credits, the portion that rating agencies could declare AAA or AA would be less. The appetite for high-rated paper, and the absence of enough high-rated companies, ensured demand for the senior, AAA or AA tranches of CDOs. Also many pension funds and other institutional investors are constrained in buying bonds to those that are (only or mostly) at least investment grade (BBB or above). This constraint helped demand for the mezzanine tranches, making the CDO system even more original and effective.

The CDO system was elaborated into CDO2 – CDOs constructed using other CDOs as the asset-backed vehicles, rather than SIVs or whatever. On to all of this were piled credit default swaps or CDSs – essentially, insurance contracts against defaults of anything at all, including often CDOs. Since an entity writing such insurance – that is, the provider of the guarantee to someone buying such a CDS – is taking on the same risk mathematically as buying an MBS, it was possible to use CDSs, written by XYZ investment bank, as the support for what were called synthetic CDOs, which could also be sold to the ravening investor community. Synthetic was a well-chosen word to describe such transactions. These wilder shores of the alphabet soup will be of great interest to Wall Street historians, and probably anthropologists, but represent more detail than is needed here.

Clearly, the competence and probity of rating agencies were central to the viability of the CDO market. No evidence on the issue of probity has yet emerged to cause the kind of trouble to the rating agencies that beset the Arthur Andersen worldwide auditing partnership after Enron imploded in 2002. However, it is likely that there will be numerous lawsuits against them by aggrieved buyers of CDOs who have suffered losses. The above examples show that the quantity of banking fees that can be taken out at the front end of the deal is extremely sensitive to the difference between the rate on the underlying mortgages and the rate end-investors will accept owing to favourable ratings. Investment bankers are not shrinking violets in pursuit of their interests. The rating agencies were under intense pressure to give favourable ratings to securities whose issuers were paying their fees.

When it comes to competence, the rating agencies are most easily criticised. Ratings such as AAA were awarded through the use of models, generally the same ones the investment banks promoting the schemes had originated. The absence of previous experience of such structures should have enforced caution. For example, mortgage brokers adopted the habit of offering piggy-back second mortgages to householders. These were basically a means of enabling the householder to do without equity: if the senior mortgage being offered was 80% of the house's value, the piggy-back, second loan would cover the remaining 20%. Yet rating agencies appear to have attached the same expected default rate to these piggy-back mortgages as to earlier-era primary mortgages. Aside from its obvious implausibility, this raises at least two questions on competence and probity:

- Should the agencies have been offering such economically significant ratings at all, given the speculative nature of the default models in utterly new and extravagant conditions?
- Were the agencies too close in interest to the sponsoring investment banks (compared with the dispersed universe of investors) to show the required disinterest in formulating a rating?

Teaser rates at the start of a mortgage

The last twist to the saga was 'teaser' rates on mortgages. Under this structure, borrowers would pay a low rate, say 4–5% below the appropriate rate for their credit, and build up the amount owed by 4–5% a year instead. Typically, the teaser period was two years, after which the enhanced principal, 108–110% of the original amount borrowed, would have to be serviced over the remaining period to the maturity of the loan. (In a typical US mortgage, this would be the remaining 28 years of the original 30.)

These teaser mortgages, to a large extent taken out by poor and often ignorant borrowers, could be passed off by the mortgage broker with the thought: 'Never mind the impact of the high payment in two years' time: house prices will have gone up and you can always refinance then with a new teaser mortgage.' Unless, of course, the mortgage market has blown up in the interim. Note the (probably sincere) assumption that house prices would go up for ever – by at least the 4–5% a year needed to keep the loan principal outstanding at or behind the value of the house that is its collateral. But house prices had stopped rising and were edging downwards from autumn 2005. After the massive contradictions of the continued growth of household mortgage debt on the assumption of ever-rising house prices had started to be appreciated, even by the artists of denial most involved in it (from February 2007), conditions on new mortgages tightened up dramatically. (Or were introduced, in the case of the ninja – no income, no job or assets – mortgages that had also been put in place, also conveniently without documentation.) The refinancing game was up, especially for the low-quality, subprime borrowers needing (as it turned out) over 100% of their home's value by way of a refinancing loan.

The rates used to illustrate these examples are based on relatively high-quality mortgages. By the time the market was forced to subsist on subprime loans as house prices plummeted from 2006 onwards, the rates were much higher – hence the need for the teaser structure to prevent borrowers from having to meet payments they could not afford in the first instance. But the packaging and SIV/CDO creation went on at the higher rates – tending to yield correspondingly higher front-end fees – as if the mortgages were going to be serviced by the borrower until maturity, though in reality, the borrower had only been hooked into the deal in the first place on the assumption that in a couple of years the house could be sold at a profit if the loan could not be refinanced at a lower rate (as soon as the teaser period was over, that is).

2

Causes and effects of the Eurasian savings glut

Causes of the gluts in various countries

Different forces in different countries led to the common result of persistent financial surpluses. In China and the Asian Tigers development strategy and policies have been crucial. Also, the orientation of development policy towards exports, though effective, leaves a domestic financial vacuum that compels unnaturally high savings rates. In the absence of either public social security or sophisticated private financial products, people have to save much more to take care of basic realities: losing their job, losing their health, getting old, buying a house, and so on. In Japan, structural business-sector behaviour now predominates. Twenty years ago excessive Japanese saving was chiefly the result of demographic shifts, which remain important. In Germany, Benelux, Scandinavia and Switzerland (north-central Europe) demography has predominated, but business restructuring has also been a factor. And, of course, business restructuring (leading to surpluses) has been significant in the US since 2001. So the balancing domestic US deficits required in government and households were even larger than the external deficit offsetting Eurasian surpluses.

In a global sense, these Eurasian surpluses have been a good example of that fashionable concept, the perfect storm. Developing Asia's mercantilism may have a greater impact relative to world GDP than similar behaviour in the heyday of Japan (1960s) or South Korea (1970s). But by itself it could probably be accommodated, along with the structural tendency towards high household savings in countries pursuing the Asian growth model. The natural tendency towards financial surplus among late-career baby-boomers, exaggerated by fears of ageing arising from rapidly growing longevity, ought to be offset by the capital spending requirements of fast growth in North America and rapid development in emerging markets. However, the latter is thwarted by the Asian export-led, high-savings model, and the possibility of simply expanding business investment to use up the spare capital is rightly rejected by businesses themselves. They have learned the lessons of the US bubble in 1998–2000 and the Japanese bubble of the late 1980s. This reinforces the shift to shareholder value and away from bureaucratic business waste. So worldwide business restructuring is the fourth element of this perfect storm of urge to surplus.

China and the Asian Tigers

In China and the Asian Tigers mercantilism remains strong, for good reasons. Excellent growth in Asia, where open-economy, export-led, high-savings policies have been adopted, contrasts starkly with dismal results in Latin America and pre-1980s India, where low savings, capital imports and import substitution created closed, siege economies. In Latin America, any move into rapid growth naturally gave rise to booming capital spending – inevitably, given major catch-up potential. With feeble domestic savings, such bursts of growth therefore required soaring imports, not just for financial reasons (that is, lack of domestic savings) but also for lack of competitive domestic capital goods industries (except perhaps construction). Such growth periods were therefore quickly choked off by debt crises as foreign lenders were discouraged by inflation and deficits, soon followed by inability or unwillingness to repay.

The import-substitution siege-economy mentality also entailed obstacles to foreign direct investment, such as domestic content quotas, dividend restraints, and so on. Meanwhile, competitiveness was further thwarted by domestic cliques and cartels carving up the protected local market. Even without these, developing the full range of industries on a small scale to supply the local market entirely loses the economies of scale that can result from focusing on a few well-chosen export industries. India remained financially sound until the 1980s, but simply grew consistently too slowly, with similar constraints.

The Pacific-Asian mercantilist approach has ensured competitive industries, because of the need to compete in export markets, and promoted economies of scale. With high savings and an export focus, capital spending needs, and the imports to supply them, have been easily financed. While the treatment of foreign capital has certainly not been uniformly free-market and transparent, China and others have encouraged direct investment to good effect in achieving rapid technology transfer and job creation.

So far, so good. But the fixation on exports and aversion to deficits became more profound as a result of the inflationary boom-bust of China in 1993–94 and – especially – the Asian crisis of 1997–98. The lack of domestic market development was paralleled by thin and inefficient financial markets and systems.

Pacific countries were humiliated as their underdeveloped financial systems collapsed under the huge inflows, followed by outflows, of global finance in the 1995–98 boom-bust. This transformed attitudes towards free capital flows. IMF policies towards South Korea and others were clearly driven more by western bank and hedge fund interests than the countries' development needs. 'Never again' entered the Asian policy vocabulary, in China as much as the countries directly affected. The resulting policies – and surpluses – have been persistent.

Japan

The source of surpluses is quite different in Japan. Demographic factors may have held up household savings rates in the past, when the large 1930s generation was in its pre-retirement phase. But now they have retired, personal savings are almost as low as America's; it is business that contributes 23–24 points of the 28–29% of GDP rate of private-sector savings. But private investment needs are less than this by 11% of GDP. Here the demographic factors remain important: both the slow growth trend of 1% or less, cutting the need for business investment, and the weakness of house-building have a lot to do with the shrinking working-age population. Private investment could well ease back further, raising the private financial surplus, unless private savings were also falling. So the private sector (unless the economy is to slump) has to run a surplus – be a net lender – of 11% of GDP.

Once again, for every surplus (lender), there is an equal and opposite deficit (borrower). Apart from the private sector, Japan has only government and foreigners as potential borrowers (that is, sources of offsetting deficits). For Japan to be close to full employment, government deficits plus current-account surpluses (that is, foreigners' borrowing) must add up to 11% of GDP. Not surprisingly, it wants as large a current surplus as possible to reduce reliance on what is already an alarming build-up of government debt. While the huge 11% private surplus may eventually dissipate, Japanese surplus pressure is unlikely to ease much in the next five years or so, as described in the main text. Certainly, right now it is if anything intensifying.

North-central Europe

European imbalances, including the NCE savings glut and the various European financial and economic disaster zones, are covered in the main text (Chapters 2, 3 and 7).

Effects of a savings glut and policy options

An excessive propensity to save in a group of countries, as described here, can lead to only a limited variety of effects or responses, outlined below and then analysed for plausibility in current conditions:

1 Higher private investment. For investment to be higher than it would be otherwise, and use up the excess saving, the required rate of return on new assets has to be driven down. It would be natural to expect such a lower rate of return if the supply of funds (saving) were boosted. In pre-Keynesian, classical economics, this is the normal, orthodox response. Wasteful private investment in Japan, and increasingly China, are examples in current conditions.

2 Lower private savings. Without any changes in public policy, a lower rate of return might also (on reasonable assumptions) be expected to lessen the attraction of private saving, whether in the glut countries or (more likely) elsewhere. Again this is a natural classical response.

3 Easier monetary policy. Easier money in non-glut countries could use up excess savings in a number of ways. First, by validating and promoting a lower real rate of interest (the fundamental cost of capital), it could induce a combination of higher investment and lower savings, provoking via policy responses 1 and 2 above. Second, where an economy is below full employment (whether or not caused by the savings glut), it could induce growth in domestic demand and net imports.

4 Easier fiscal policy. Government can directly dis-save or invest, offsetting the savings glut, by shifting towards deficit financing. (This was John Maynard Keynes's last-resort remedy in the Depression, and Keynesians' first-resort remedy for any slowdown since 1945.)

5 Depression of demand, income and output. If none of the above occur on a sufficient scale, the potential savings glut will express itself as deficient demand, lowering output and incomes to the level where the saving out of such income is no longer higher than investment. The investment in such scenarios generally includes a large measure of unwanted inventory, as sales falling short of businesses' expectations. This inventory hangover lowers future demand – that is, raises further the potential savings surplus. Demand, income and output enter a downward spiral. This may be checked by a build-up of involuntary, cyclical government deficits as tax revenue falls and relief spending rises.

The story here is of how various combinations of the first

four responses, in various countries, have enabled the fifth to be avoided until the recent crisis – and of how a risk of depression, or liquidity trap, still exists, especially in continental Europe. The story has already been suggested in the analysis of the meaning of excessive saving – the propensity to save, so-called *ex ante* saving, cannot be directly measured, as saving is known only after the event, *ex post*. As measured after the event, saving always equals investment. (Investment is demand or output less consumption; saving is income less consumption; so by definition, demand, income and output are equal.) The saving that people wish to do *ex ante* can only be the subject of conjecture. It is through the presence of responses 1–4 above that the excess in *ex ante* saving can be inferred.

The US economy, which has been the central user of excessive Eurasian savings, initiated responses 1–4 in that order. First, there was higher investment in the late 1990s bubble, with a wealth effect that induced lower personal savings. Second, when the bubble burst, the Fed slashed interest rates, reinforcing the fall in personal savings by inducing huge increases in borrowing (rather than lower contractual savings in such vehicles as pension funds and mortgage repayments). The large 2001 tax cut (response 3) came close behind. When the stockmarket and economy contin-ued to languish during 2002 the approach was more of the same: another large tax and interest-rate cut in 2003 to reinforce the 'Baghdad bounce'. The result was been 4–5 years of boom with the housing and debt bubbles ending in the recent crisis. Essen-tially, since the 1998–2000 bubble, the US has dis-saved to match the excess savings elsewhere (response 4).

Why 'invest more' did not work: the bubble, 1998–2000

The story starts with the Asian crisis of 1997–98. 'Irrational exuberance' was Alan Greenspan's verdict on the US stockmarket before it all started, in December 1996. The S&P index was at 740. At the peak of the bubble, three and a half years later in spring/summer 2000, it had more than doubled to 1,520. The Nasdaq 100 index – the centre of tech-bubble folly – had gone up 5½ times over the same period, from 840 to 4,700. How did Greenspan react to this huge increment of irrationality and exuberance? He encouraged it. Why? At least in part as an indirect response to the 1997 Asian crisis, and its aftermath, the massive flow of Asian funds (and repatriated US speculative capital) to the US safe haven. The heavy flow of European capital to the US began at about the same time, but was smaller and less of a policy concern.

Increases of interest rates to quell irrational exuberance were put on hold in 1997 at least in part to avoid reinforcing the already devastating financial consequences of the Asian crisis. In late 1998, in mid-boom for the US and Europe, the grossly heightened speculative fever arising from excessive cheap funding (conspicuously in yen, as a severe recession was in progress in Japan in parallel with the Asian crisis) led to the spectacular bankruptcy of Long Term Capital Management, with Russian financial collapse and default its contingent cause. Greenspan cut US interest rates three times in seriously misconceived or at least exaggerated anxiety over liquidity. This fuelled the last stage of the stratospheric rise of the stockmarket and the economy.

The increase in underlying profitability in US business was the true source of strength in the 1990s stockmarket. But it was largely over by the end of 1994: non-financial companies' pre-tax return on net worth nearly doubled from 5½% in 1990–91 to over 9% by the last quarter of 1994. It had little to do with high-tech, which had been just as powerful an innovative factor in the 1980s, when profitability changed little, and again in the mid to late 1990s, when it fell. The drive after 1990 for shareholder value was the cause of improved profitability, arising (as in Japan after 1997) from restructuring. This cost cutting probably owed most to the attack on bureaucratic business management practices by the 'policemen' of capitalism: Mike Milken, Carl Icahn, T. Boone Pickens and the like (see Chapter 2).

The search for shareholder value was reinforced by the high cost of borrowing after the turnaround to lower inflation caused by the stringent monetary policy of Paul Volcker. Hostile takeovers may not have generated much improvement in overall shareholder value in many instances, but the fear of predators certainly changed behaviour in the managements that survived. This is the Admiral Byng effect, in memory of a British admiral who was shot on a ship's quarterdeck for losing Minorca in 1756; Voltaire remarked that the British 'put an admiral to death now and then, to encourage the others'.

Once the US corporate return on equity reached 9%, the natural reaction of businesses was to want more assets on which to earn such returns. Capital spending had been leading the 1990s economic advance since mid-1992, soon after the start of the upswing of profitability. By 1997, the five-year growth rate of real business capital expenditure had reached 10%. Kingsley Amis, a British novelist, once (in a different context) remarked: 'More means worse.' Economists talk of diminishing returns. It is no coincidence that pre-tax returns to equity, having been on a plateau of around 9% from late 1994 to 1997, relapsed, just as the capital expenditure growth rate achieved double figures, and stayed there for two and a half years until the bubble burst in mid-2000.

After the dire experience of 1998–2002, culminating in the Enron crisis and high junk debt yields, US businesses abandoned any thoughts of wasteful investment for good. The run-up of non-financial business debt in 2006–07, when it took a slight lead over dubious mortgages as the source of extra private-sector non-financial borrowing, was mostly to buy back shares (in leveraged buy-outs and as a means of distributing profits without committing to higher dividends), not to invest in unnecessary capital assets. Then in the recent crisis, businesses, still on the alert, front-led the recession with cuts in capital spending.

This experience argues against one plausible response to such savings flows: that the West should use the funds to invest more – to store the benefit of the inflows for the future, for example to take care of future pension funding needs as populations age. The fallacy is that such investment almost by definition carries an inadequate return. (Otherwise the savings could not be considered excessive.) It can therefore only happen in the private sector in a context in which normal return expectations are distorted by a financial bubble, giving the illusion of strong returns when they are actually falling.

Only if economies (or societies) lower their expectations of reasonable investment returns can the invest-more policy work. But this creates two problems. First, requiring strong returns is a crucial condition of healthy economic development, and should not be abandoned because of peculiarities of savings behaviour in other societies. Second, the foreign savings inflows tend to drive up asset prices, at least initially, raising expectations of easy capital gains – the reverse of the lowered expectations that are more appropriate. The only plausible source for an invest-more policy is the government. This sort of policy, advocated by Keynes in the Depression, was adopted by Japan in the 1990s after its late 1980s bubble. Japan's legendary waste and corruption in public projects illustrate the severe limits on such an invest-more approach. Once capital ceases to be perceived as scarce and costly, and starts being thrown around indiscriminately, the hoped-for returns from investment melt away.

Lower private savings: inflation of asset prices – the bubble wealth effect

Personal savings rates, paradoxically, do not necessarily go down because of lower interest rates. In an economy with little or no personal holdings of real assets other than owner-occupied homes, low real interest rates might require households to increase savings. Suppose people wished to reach age 65 with some form of pension pot. If real interest rates were low, the savings rate would need to be higher to accumulate the pot. Low real returns would cause low annuity rates after the age of 65, the pension payout period, so a larger pot would anyhow be required for a given desired rate of pension (relative to previous earned income). Thus lower real rates would force both a higher proportionate savings rate for a given pot and a larger pot for a given ratio of eventual pension to previous income, both of which would tend to result in higher savings. Conversely, higher real rates would permit a given ratio of eventual pension to current salary at a lower rate of saving. This idea is uncomfortable for classical economics, as it means that offering a lower rate of return tends to increase savings, and vice versa.

Introduce personal holdings of equities, a build-up of Eurasian surpluses flowing into (chiefly) America and the bubble, and some things become clearer, others less so. How is the rate of return lowered by the inflow of surpluses? By rising asset prices: the bubble. For savers with existing asset holdings, the achievement of a desired pension pot is advanced at a stroke by rising stockmarket prices. So although the rate of return has been lowered, the all-in return to existing asset-holders has received a boost. This higher all-in rate of return acts like the higher real rates described above: by making the pot more easily achieved, it lowers the need to save. This is the wealth effect, leading to a lower savings rate.

This deals with only half of the problem, however. The lower real returns resulting from soaring asset prices mean that the annuity or pension payable from a given pot will be lower (especially given increasing longevity). This implies a rising pot – evidence being widely publicised and large shortfalls in US and UK company pension plans on proper calculations. It is hard to resist the conclusion that US households adopted an ostrich-like or Micawber strategy on this (hoping something will turn up). It looks like a case of inverted Alzheimer's disease. In the real Alzheimer's, old people forget the past. With inverted Alzheimer's, middle-aged people forget the future.

The fundamental point of this book is that it is the Eurasian surpluses that have trashed household balance sheets, and thereby created the danger of a liquidity trap. For the most part, this is an argument about excessive household debt and borrowing. But

complacency about the size of pension pot needed to meet promises and expectations also suggests a major problem arising from
lower rates of return on the asset side of personal balance sheets.
This mostly concerns America and Britain, rather than continental Europe. It is the Anglo-Saxons who have much the greater
reliance on private pension funds, rather than tax-financed public
provision with an overlay of private wealth. The resulting equity
culture means the wealth effect on saving has been far greater
in America and Britain. Continental Europeans have their own
peculiar exposure to a huge rise in taxation to fund extravagant
public pension promises. But the Anglo-Saxons, via public insurance vehicles to make up for private pension scheme failures, may
well find themselves too with unexpectedly large tax increases on
account of widespread failures in private provision.

Post-bubble monetary and fiscal ease

This book covers the key aspects of monetary and fiscal ease
that have persistently attempted to offset the Eurasian surpluses.
Broadly, monetary ease fuelled the private-sector debt crisis,
whereas fiscal ease obviously does the same for government
debt. The fundamental point is simple. With a major portion of
the world's economies running structural surpluses, the countries
running the corresponding deficits can only achieve reasonable,
that is, on-trend growth with moderate inflation, for example
2–3%, at the expense of rising debt ratios that will eventually
prove intolerable.

3

How financial regulation might be changed

What looked in late 2008 like Wall Street privatising the government now seems likely to be reversed under popular pressure. The furore over bankers' bonuses illustrated one aspect of recent financial market conduct that has wide implications: the casual slippage back to normalcy, interpreted as business-as-usual, 2007-style. But normalcy is a long way off. Indeed, complacency in many quarters about economic recovery, and the illusion of normalcy, is itself a reason why renewed economic and financial trouble, possibly crisis, is likely. The drop in bank shares on the announcement of new regulatory plans by President Obama, originated by a former Fed governor, Paul Volcker, was a classic case of blinkers falling from the eyes of financial markets that have been amazingly credulous and deluded in recent years (if not always). Remember the Latin American debt farrago ('countries can't go bankrupt'), the high-leverage, saving-and-loans bubble, the tech bubble, as much as the recent alphabet-soup mortgage bubble. These were obvious cases where a little scepticism, and willingness to look at situations from multiple perspectives, seemed to be beyond the reach of market participants, or their educators. But it would have saved them a lot of money, and made bank shares more, not less, valuable.

Proposals to restructure the financial system should be subject to a number of tests:

- Do they address clear weaknesses revealed by the recent crisis?
- Do they neglect (or even worsen) problems so revealed?
- Do they secure other worthwhile goals?
- Do they cause collateral damage?

To relate changes to such questions raises the question of what did cause the recent crisis. Clearly, this goes beyond bad behaviour by the 'banksters'. Mistakes and perverted behaviour patterns occurred on the part of borrowers, lenders and intermediaries. And the whole fabric of finance was rent by the tension arising from economic imbalances – the complementary 25-year leveraging up of America and the Eurasian savings glut.

It is reasonable to look to regulation to minimise the chances of another surge of dubious lending, as in subprime mortgages – at their extreme, the ninja (no income, no job or assets) mortgages. But this means cutting into the pathology of the supply-driven market. Regarding the ultimate source of supply – the Eurasian savings glut, which flooded the world with cheap money as excess saving naturally reduced the return on capital – regulation is powerless. But the alphabet soup of derivatives that enabled blatantly unsuitable mortgages to be written and placed with apparently sophisticated investors was crucial to the activities of the mortgage brokers that originated the deals. That style of business arose in part because the securities industry operates simultaneously as a marketmaker – underwriting and placing securities and derivatives – and dealer in the same securities and derivatives.

This natural conflict is exacerbated in its impact by the remuneration system that encourages bad faith on the part of such broker-dealers in pursuing their own interests, not merely to the neglect of their clients but also at their expense. The financial industry showed no self-restraint whatever in its pursuit of such bad-faith profits. Indeed, the payout of bonuses that reflected the large spread between the rates on the underlying mortgages and the low cost of borrowing (courtesy of the savings glut) reflected a conflict between extremely clever bankers and their own (generally less clever) shareholders.

Before considering how the new Obama/Volcker plan addresses this central issue, the other question that any reform needs to address is how to minimise the risk of a repeat of the Lehman situation (and its predecessor, Bear Stearns), in which large but by no means dominant financial players became too big to fail.

The new plan is conceived to reduce banking conflicts that the market has shown itself unable to self-regulate, and indirectly to create natural curbs on excessive remuneration. At the same time it avoids the widely touted return to Glass-Steagall, which would be highly destructive in view of financial market innovations, especially since the 1980s, but arguably dating from the flotation of the dollar in 1971. To be effective, the proposals should also require continued, relatively intrusive regulatory oversight, and that is all to the good.

There is an obvious conflict between banks holding own-account positions in key markets where they are also the leading marketmakers making prices for clients. It is not just a question of front-running, where a dealer positions his own account first, and then moves the price in his favour by putting through a large client transaction. More dangerous are the situations amusingly detailed in Michael Lewis's *Liar's Poker*, where a bank wishing to shed a position sets its sales force to work to stuff them into a client's book by outright lying. Even without such foul play, a marketmaking bank that deals with major client flows, even, for example, with central banks, has a major advantage over other investors, and should not be able to engage in large-scale profitable trading off that.

Policing the distinction between own-account trading and legitimate hedging of positions taken as a result of marketmaking for a client is clearly going to be difficult and inevitably somewhat arbitrary. It will also require close regulatory oversight – a good thing in itself, since the financial industry has for too long lived in a solipsistic, self-referencing world that precludes self-discipline. Close policing may not solve some of the inevitable arbitrariness of the new distinction, but it should ensure that the development of bubble-like excesses is spotted and thwarted a little earlier than has been typical in recent years.

For banks' shareholders, the forcing out of own-account trading into separate organisations is all to the good. Under the arrangements of recent decades, diffuse shareholders of banks have been hopelessly out-gunned by the greatest capitalists in the history of the world: their employees. Yet the profits accruing from bankers' activities on behalf of their firms are mostly to the credit of the firm, not the employee. Many were the employees who left my old firm, JPMorgan, to work for themselves; and almost as many were the ones who soon came back to the comfort zone of JPMorgan. It was – and remains – largely the JPMorgan name, balance sheet, support system and reputation that made the money, not the employee. If a person wants to make the sort of money that was wrongly being handed out at quite low levels in such banks in recent years, they should go it alone, as a hedge fund for example. The only people who should get rewards on the recent scale are the ones who really make a difference: the senior management that genuinely does create the reputation, operating culture and organisation of the firm.

The new regulations, by sharply limiting the scope for traders and others within regulated banks to run books and claim undue credit for their profits, should force out the ones wishing to make huge rewards to set up their own businesses – while those that stay 'in the warm' get the good but not immoderate pay that they deserve. While the original Volcker proposal was to ban own-account trading by banks making markets for clients, this will not work in practice. Apart from anything else, the largest issuance and trading market right now, and probably for a while in future, is and will be government bonds (given the size of their deficits). But it is not possible to be a dealer in government bonds and provide proper service to clients without some degree of positioning on one's own account, simply to avoid getting caught on the wrong foot by foreseeable shifts. So the better regulatory approach is not to ban such own-account trading, but to make it subject to high capital requirements.

Good traders will always be taking more risk than most in a bank, and so should be comparatively well paid, but recent rewards have been excessive and unnecessary. So it is far from clear that these proposals are bad for bank shareholders, as opposed to the employees who have been getting huge bonuses. The negative stockmarket reaction to the original Volcker proposals may have been dominated, as often, by the interests of the bankers rather than the owners of the banks.

The Volcker proposals were unnecessarily strict on banks holding interests in hedge funds. Provided banks do so at holding-company level, outside the regulated subsidiaries that should contain the bulk of the business and capital of the firm, and with Chinese walls to prevent any organisational links between the hedge fund management and the operating banking subsidiaries, it is hard to see the objection – beyond some overall limit on the relative size of such holdings. A better line to take in terms of preventing conflicts of interest might be to question the ownership by banks of asset management subsidiaries – this has led to identifiable conflicts of interest, including in high-profile mergers and acquisition deals.

It would be a mistake if the likes of Goldman Sachs and Morgan Stanley could escape all this by giving up their banking charters and reverting to investment bank status. It would ignore the point that balance sheet size was what created the Lehman disaster, given the intricate web of derivatives that will under any future scenario link deposit-taking banks and other financial institutions inextricably together. The argument against Glass-Steagall in modern conditions, and some other recent narrow banking proposals to separate safe bread-and-butter banks from riskier institutions, is precisely that conventional banking activities (in the Glass-Steagall sense) now inevitably are accompanied by associated derivative and other hedging activities. These are in themselves – as naked positions – just as risky as anything that was banished from conventional commercial banking to the investment banking arena under Glass-Steagall. So that kind of risk-taking is inherent to modern banking, including the basic provision of loans, and has been ever since the invention of the interest-rate swap in the early 1980s (if not the emergence of floating exchange rates in the 1970s). Equally, investment bankers now have to be able to offer such swaps, and other long-lasting derivatives, that require credit exposures and thus a large, healthy balance sheet – hence the convergence of commercial and investment banking over the past 30 years.

All institutions with a balance sheet of significant size need to be regulated, if the Lehman-type scenario is to be minimised. Just as importantly, it should be a priority to insist that the new, presumably higher and safer, required levels of regulatory capital are kept within the subsidiaries that engage in the transactions the capital is supposed to support. If this incidentally stops a lot of tax-dodging by banks holding their capital in tax havens while the deals are done in major capitals, so much the better – it is the taxpayers in the major capitals that have had to bail them out.

The lack of international co-ordination, lamented in some quarters, was always hankering after a chimera. A strong lead from a man like Volcker is so obviously vastly superior to prolonged negotiations with a bunch of politically motivated bureaucrats, who do not understand and often dislike finance in the first place, that we should all emit a sigh of relief. Eurasian savings-glut countries will have to address the great difficulties their behaviour pattern will increasingly entail. But the onus for altering delinquent banking behaviour clearly lies with America.

Bibliography

Bernanke, B., 'The Global Savings Glut and the US Current Account Deficit', Sandridge Lecture, Virginia Association of Economics, March 2005.

Dumas, C. and Choyleva, D., *The Bill from the China Shop: How Asia's Savings Glut Threatens the World Economy*, Profile Books, 2006.

Dumas, C., *China and America: A Time of Reckoning*, Profile Books, 2008.

Dumas, C., 'US balance sheets serially trashed by Eurasian surplus', Lombard Street Research, *Monthly International Review*, No. 143, September 30th, 2004 (available on request from the author).

Friedman, M. and Schwarz, A., *A Monetary History of the United States, 1867–1960*, Princeton University Press, 1963.

Keynes, J.M., *The General Theory of Employment, Interest and Money*, Macmillan Cambridge University Press, 1936.

Reading, B., *Japan: The Coming Collapse*, Weidenfeld and Nicholson, 1992.

Schumpeter, J., *Capitalism, Socialism and Democracy*, Harper & Row, 1942.

Shiller, R., *Animal Spirits: How Human Psychology Drives the Economy and Why It Matters for Global Capitalism*, Princeton University Press, March 2009.

Shiller, R., *Subprime Solution: How Today's Global Financial Crisis Happened and What to Do about It*, Princeton University Press, September 2008.

Smithers, A., *Wall Street Revalued: Imperfect Markets and Inept Central Bankers*, John Wiley & Sons, 2009.

Wolf, M., *Why Globalisation Works*, Yale University Press, 2005.

Wolf, M., *Fixing Global Finance: How to Curb Financial Crisis in the 21st Century*, The Johns Hopkins University Press, 2008.

Index